Success University for Women™ in Leadership (Volume III)
Library of Congress Cataloging-in-Publication Date
available upon request
ISBN-13:978-1978257573
ISBN-10:1978257570
Publishers: *Success University for Women*™, LLC
Designer: Helen Scarth, Stuf² Incorporated {*www.stuf2.com*}
Editorial Assistants: Jennie Ritchie, Amy Sawchenko
Cover Photo/Interior Photograph by Joseph Marable
{*www.jomarweddingphotography.com*}

To order this title, please visit:
www.successuniversityforwomen.com

To bring a *Success University for Women*™ conference or speaker to your area, please email:
info@successuniversityforwomen.com

Success University for Women™ in Leadership

Created by

Jan Fraser and Catherine Scheers

written with successful women from around the world

Here's to the shatterers of glass ceilings, to the women who led the way, both famous and those on whom the limelight has not yet shone.

Contents

Contents

Contents

Praise for Success University for Women™ in Leadership

"The authors of **Success University for Women™ in Leadership** share their inspirational—and often vulnerable—life stories, empowering other women to take the chance and let their brilliance shine! Women mentoring women is the most natural expression of who we are. Let these stories transform your life and lead you into your heart where real leadership success happens. If you are ready to be one of the new women who are inspired, empowered and enlightened leaders of our time. This book is a must read for you."

Sandra Biskind
International #1 Best-selling Author of the **CODEBREAKER PLATINUM** *Series, Speaker and Private Consultant to Transformational leaders and entrepreneurs*

"Be prepared to be inspired, challenged, and bedazzled. The stories on these pages about each author's journey will give you hope, and stir in you the conviction that impossible is nothing! *Success University for Women™ in Leadership* is your roadmap to creating even greater successes. It will restore faith in your capacity to be the leader others want to follow. And if you're on the fence about the direction you need to take, you will surely find the answers in these pages as well."

Rani St. Pucchi
Award-winning Designer, Bestselling Author, Image Consultant, Inspirational Speaker and Coach
www.ranistpucchi.com

Praise for Success University for Women™ in Leadership

"The Dalai Lama said, "The Western Woman will change the world." Here are world-changers, leaders—women who are reaching out to other women to lift them up, provide them knowledge, and encourage them on their path of leadership. I'm honored to know many of the authors in this book. Their experience, vulnerability and integrity shine through their chapters. The world needs more conscious women leaders—this book is for you."

Dr. Anita L. Sanchez
Speaker and Author of the International Best-seller, **The Four Sacred Gifts: Indigenous Wisdom for Modern Times**

Success University for Women™ has done it again! A new, powerful book about leadership. These compelling stories will inform you about the skills and actions needed to be a leader, and will inspire you to believe that yes, you too have everything it takes to step into leadership! A great book by amazing women who focus their personal power to make the world a better place!

Deborah Sandella PhD, RN
#1 International Best-selling Author of **Goodbye Hurt & Pain, 7 Simple Steps to Health, Love and Success,** (Conari Press)
Creator of RIM—an unprecedented organic technique to quickly shed toxic emotions from your body

Praise for Success University for Women™ *in Leadership*

"Leaders today need to understand what it takes to build an unstoppable team. I would recommend *Success University for Women*™ *in Leadership* to anyone looking for ways to improve their leadership capabilities and master the art of team building."

Dori DeCarlo
Founder Safety Bags, Inc. and Word of Mom Radio Host
www.StadiumBags.com

"I am delighted to see a book focused on inspiring women to use their strengths to lead. A must read for any woman looking to achieve professional and personal success."

Julie Nelsen
Assistant Professor, St. Catherine University (the largest college for women in the United States)

"The authors in this book have an amazing capacity to inspire others to be a better version of themselves. Kathleen Seeley has converted her deep knowledge of values-based leadership into rare wisdom and delivers her message with humour and candour to corporate and private audiences alike. A gifted teacher, I am honoured to have been one of those in the audience who have been guided by her expertise and wisdom."

Lauren Evanow
CEO, JITGA (Just in Time Genius Assistant)

Praise for Success University for Women™ in Leadership

"I highly recommend *Success University for Women™ in Leadership* as it connects with readers both young and old in shaping new viewpoints and shifting requirements in their respective domains of influence. It is a passionately penned book containing fresh and new ideas for a practical everyday reference guide."

Cheryl Griffith
Programme Director, Women of Purpose Ministry, Barbados

"Powerful and honest in its writing, this is a wonderful read full of unique answers to tough questions. A must read for women seeking to expand their leadership skills with integrity, and in accordance to their highest values."

Casandra Gally
Clinical Psychologist

"A leader must recognize that he or she is working for the common good of those they have been called to serve. *Success University for Women™ in Leadership* is a must read for business owners and leaders looking to gain a competitive edge."

L. Laraia
VP Director of Marketing

Praise for Success University for Women™ in Leadership

"This book is encouraging for women who are aspiring to be a leader or for those who are already in leadership positions. Its broad coverage of topics and leadership arenas make it a treasure for any woman moving forward in her career and life."

Jennifer Bettis-Jones
CEO, North County Martial Arts, Carlsbad, CA

"Jam-packed with inspiration for business owners who want to make a difference. From how to motivate and mentor to making a connection and leaving a legacy they nailed it!"

Tammy Valenti Ladd
Owner, The Chameleon Salon & Color Studio

in Leadership

Created by Jan Fraser and Catherine Scheers
Contributing Authors (In Alphabetical Order)

J.L. (Jani) Ashmore
Dina Blanco-Ioannou
Nannette Bosh
Marie-Jo Caesar
Giselle Commissiong
Derra Edwards
Tracy Isaak
Diane Polnow
Lanette Pottle
Tracy Quinn
Natasha Ryan
Kathleen Seeley
Colleen Sorensen
Kristi Staab
Agatha Starczyk
Bronwen Talley-Coffey
Gale Weithers
Deanna Won

this is what I can do in Africa with Touch the Sky.

Disclaimer

ounded in 2015 by Jan Fraser and Catherine Scheers, *Success University for Women*™ is an organization whose vision is to educate, empower, and promote women around the world through books, conferences, and courses.

This book shares individual author's lessons learned the hard way, through life, through mistakes, by searching for answers, reading books, taking courses, finding mentors, and learning a better way. We are honored to share their stories with you.

The stories you are about to read are each author's personal experience and opinion. Any sharing of personal information or names is at their discretion. The authors' challenges and victories are their unique experiences. We make no claims that you will experience exactly the same results.

Success University for Women™ is not a post-secondary institution. While we offer training, workshops, and conferences to educate, empower, and promote women, and a process to obtain your Certificate of Completion at the end of this book, we do not promise you a two or four year university degree.

May you find inspiration and motivation in these stories to uplift, encourage, and direct your path.

Touch the Sky! workshops and conferences and retreats-

Dedication

*T*his book is dedicated to every woman who stepped up to lead and influence us, sacrificing greatly at times, to ensure we were ready to take a renewed and greater role in all areas of our lives. These women *were* and *are* in our homes, communities, and the world.

In the history of civilization, women's primary roles have been child bearers and homemakers. They have not traditionally been viewed as leaders. However, in the last 400 years, and especially in the last 100, more and more women are stepping into the limelight as leaders.

These well-known women are leading the way in many areas of business and culture, providing leadership models for millions of women and girls around the world. You will see the names of these leaders on 'word cloud' diagrams in each section of this book.

Take time to thank them as well as leaders in your personal experience, for blazing the trail, courageously leading the way, and bravely breaking stereotypes to make a real difference in the world.

Thank you for leading by example.

Jan Fraser   Catherine Scheers

Co-Founders, *Success University for Women*™

Acknowledgement

*T*his book could not have taken shape without the love and trust that our co-authors placed in our hands. Thank you for never losing sight of our vision to educate, empower, and promote women throughout the world, and for co-creating this volume with us.

Many thanks to our talented designer, Helen Scarth of Stuf² Incorporated {*www.stuf2.com*}. Sincere thanks also to our Editorial Assistants: Jennie Ritchie and Amy Sawchenko and photographer Joe Marable.

To all our readers, friends, followers, and conference attendees—thank you for catching the vision and getting excited about empowering women around the globe. Thank you for sharing the message with others through social media, within your companies and with your friends. This third book would not be possible without your energy and encouragement.

To the various co-workers, supervisors, organizations, and mentors who inspired the stories in this book—thank you for the lessons that we now pass along to others.

To our husbands, Ian Coles and Chris Scheers—thank you for your love, advice, patience and the space to create *Success University for Women*™ *in Leadership* (*Volume III*). Thank you for being on this incredible journey with us.

Jan   *Catherine*

Foreword

Darlene Whitehurst

Darlene Whitehurst is President and Chief Creative Officer of am3 adsource (Adsource Media, Inc.), a full-service brand and promotions agency located in Raleigh, North Carolina.

Adsource Media, Inc. is celebrating its 19th year in business as a 100% Woman Owned and Operated Business specializing in integrated marketing campaigns, branded merchandise and consumer engagement programs. Darlene is the recipient of multiple awards including recognition for *Supplier Diversity Leadership* and advancing women in business, industry and the community.

For more information visit:
www.am3adsource.com

Foreword

by Darlene Whitehurst

*T*he topic of women in leadership roles has never been more timely. Although women have "Come a long way, Baby," as the ad executives tell us, we still have miles to go to advance from "secretary to CEO."

How do we begin to address this issue? Women helping women! That is the premise of this book and it is also the basis for my company, GoalFriends. The authors of **Success University for Women™ in Leadership** share their stories in an authentic and vulnerable way so that other women can learn from their journey. GoalFriends is a personal growth network of women supporting women in obtaining their dreams and goals. That's why I'm proud to introduce this book to you.

I share a mentor with the Co-Founders of this book, Jan Fraser and Catherine Scheers, and with many of the authors of this book. We have been fortunate to study with someone I call the 'Male Oprah'—Jack Canfield. Jack is the Co-Founder of the incredibly successful **Chicken Soup for the Soul®** franchise of books, author of **The Success Principles™** and holds the world record for the most books on the New York Times Best-Seller list at one time! The fact that he wrote the foreword for *Success University for Women*™ *(Volume 1)* speaks to the credibility of these women.

Whether you are already a leader, or if you are just starting out and want someone to light the way, this book is for you. You will laugh and cry, you will gasp and take a deep breath, as I did when I read these stories. The authors show that leadership requires grit and determination.

Let them lead and inspire you on your journey of further transformation and success.

See you at the top!

Darlene Whitehurst
Founder of GoalFriends
President and Chief Creative Officer of Adsource Media, Inc.

Preface

Preface

Are you...a leader or aspire to be one? Searching for a leadership mentor that has been where you are? Embarking on a more significant leadership role?

*I*n *Success University for Women*™ *in Leadership* (Volume III), 20 leaders from six countries around the world address these questions and more. Our Success Sisters hail from industries as varied as sales, accounting, aerospace, education, health care, hotel management, human resources, insurance, the military, professional development, and the arts.

These authors have all faced career challenges that they overcame to become leaders. They come from all walks of life—some are younger, some more seasoned; some are introverts, others extroverts; career women and entrepreneurs; mothers, grandmothers and women without children. They faced losses and they've had victories. Their occupations differ wildly; they reside all around the world, their ages range from the 30's to the 70's. Yet they have encountered similar struggles—in health,

Preface

love, careers, money, and with family. You may see your own challenges reflected in their stories.

Let their experiences and guidance empower you in your leadership quest.

About this Book

This book is divided into four sections for ease in navigation. Section One is *Transforming*. The authors in this section share how they transformed themselves to become leaders others want to follow.

Section Two is *Inspiring*. Regardless of where you are in your career path, these authors show by their example how to inspire others—the true mark of a leader.

Section Three is *Unifying*. The right leadership can make or break a team. Learn from these authors how to create a successful team to support you in your career.

Section Four is *Influencing*. The experienced leaders in this section share their strategies for positively influencing others.

Check the Table of Contents for the topics in each chapter. Dive into the section or chapter that speaks to your particular situation, then come back around and read the others.

At the end of each chapter, you'll find the author's *Success University for Women*™ *'Success Strategies.'* These *'Success Strategies'* summarize their chapter and give you words of wisdom to guide you on your own journey.

After you have read these stories, and incorporated this 'curriculum' into your life, you will be ready to graduate from *Success University for Women*™.

Preface

All convocations come with a certificate—instructions for receiving yours is included in the back of this book.

Congratulations, Graduate!
Apply what you learn here, and you will be well on your way to success in life!

Section One

Transforming

Can I look up the women whose names I do not know? are there 50 names here?

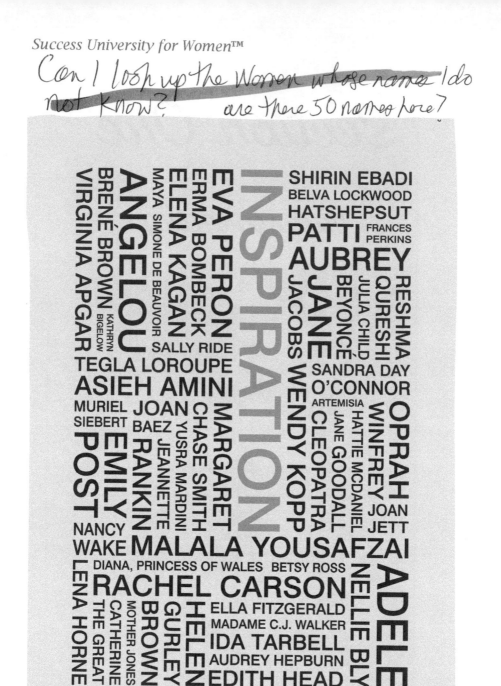

SECTION ONE: INTRODUCTION

*T*o be a leader, we must first lead ourselves. We need to know and trust our values, purpose, strengths and yes, weaknesses, before others will trust us. When we walk our talk, lead by example and demonstrate the behaviours we want from others, our leadership is irresistible to others.

In this section, you'll learn strategies for leading and transforming yourself so that you may lead others.

Success University for Women™ Co-Founder *Catherine Scheers* demonstrates the benefits of emotional intelligence when dealing with difficult situations in your career. Leadership expert *Kathleen Seeley* of Canada shows us the importance of values-based leadership—knowing and sticking to your values amidst life's storms. Switzerland's *Dina Blanco-Ioannou* called upon great strength in breaking cultural barriers and creating a new career that inspires herself and her clients. *Tracy Quinn* also pushed through roadblocks on her way to success, using feedback and passion to fuel her career. Seattle's *Natasha Ryan* gives you a strategy to break through barriers en route to the top. Toronto-based *Giselle Commissiong* reveals how quickly admitting a major misstep allowed her to find her purpose and excel in her career.

These authors transparently share their struggles and successes, and the strategies they used to become leaders in their careers.

These chapters will help you establish yourself as someone others want to follow.

Catherine Scheers

Catherine Scheers is a professional speaker and best-selling author who helps corporations maximize their employees' potential. She is Co-Founder of *Success University for Women*™ and Co-Author of the international best-sellers **Success University for Women™ in Business (Volume II), Success University for Women™ (Volume I)** and **The Success Secret**.

Catherine is a Canfield *Success Principles*™ Trainer, Certified Professional Success Coach and graduate of the University of Calgary (B.A. Communications, Honours).

As someone who has held several highly stressful positions, from corporate to entrepreneurial, Catherine has a big heart for helping others overcome stress. Through her *Stress to Bliss*™ Workshops, she helps women to release their stress and re-charge their lives.

www.empoweringsuccess.ca

SECTION ONE: CHAPTER ONE

Emotional Leadership

by Catherine Scheers

> *"I would like to be known as an intelligent woman, a courageous woman, a loving woman, a woman who teaches by being."* Maya Angelo

"We love you! We really love you! We want you to stay, but...we have given the job to another candidate."

I felt the sucker punch deep in my gut. The president of our non-profit organization was informing me that although I was acting director for the past three months, and a flourishing internal candidate for my current job, I was unsuccessful in the formal application. In those three months, I had worked 60 to 70 hours per week, and had been successful internally and with donors. Candidates were paraded by my office to be interviewed; my self-worth wobbled with each fleeting comparison as they passed by the office I would soon have to vacate. As the president waited far too long for my reply, I sputtered, "I'm open-minded and willing to work with the new director." These calm sentiments belayed my inner turmoil.

Keep calm and soldier on

> *"The truth is, everything will be okay as soon as you are okay with everything. And that's the only time everything will be OK." Michael Singer*

Mortified by the impending embarrassment of not securing my own job, I calmly walked out of the office, assailed by thoughts: 'Did I mess up in the job?' No, the president had gone out of his way to let me know that was not the case. 'What does that person have that I don't have?' He had experience and accomplishments in former fundraising roles. 'How will we manage with a smaller salary with my husband currently unemployed?'

With each thought, my mood dived and my head hurt. There was only one cure—wine and whine.

Do you want to be happy or not?

As I poured my heart out to my husband, and he poured the wine for me, all these thoughts and feelings tumbled out of my mouth and heart.

After the fear and humiliation passed, I was left with this one question: 'Do you want to be happy or not?' I could accept the inevitable with grace, or be a sore loser. Either way, change was inevitable. I needed an attitude adjustment!

Clarity

Getting perspective on a situation can often help us to accept an outcome. A little game I like to play is, 'It Could Be Worse!' For example, if you have a minor fender-bender accident, you could say, 'It could be worse...an elephant could have sat on my car!' Make your 'it could be worse' statement as ridiculous as possible for a little humour.

As for me, it could have been worse...they could have fired me! Or, it could be worse...they could have hired a giraffe, and then I would have a sore neck from looking up!

Control your emotions

"A diamond is a chunk of coal that did well under pressure." Anonymous

Women often get a bad reputation for crying in the office. They are made to feel less valuable because they show emotion.

One way of avoiding the label of 'emotional female' is to focus on the facts as if you were a lawyer. As Joe Friday used to say, "Just the facts, Ma'am!" You may feel those feelings, but you must focus on dispassionate particulars while you are there.

Put on your poker face and save the tears for home. Once home, do a little soul searching. Identify the specific emotions you were feeling. They can give you a clue as to why you are upset. Are you feeling panic? Where is it coming from? Or sadness...what is making you sad?

Being specific can be empowering, versus the 'everything sucks' generalization. Specificity can lead to strategies to change things in the future.

An emotion I am trying to tame is anger. I am quick to flame and a long, slow burner. This does not help me in the office. When someone challenges me, I get angry, just like anyone else. Yet I try to control that anger, rather than react to it. Let me be very clear: this is NOT easy. I have a black-belt in sarcasm, and as a mom of five, I can stop people with a look.

However difficult it may be to change your communication patterns, it is a lot easier than alienating your co-workers and/or looking for another job if you let your temper get the best of you. Whenever my quick tongue gets ahead of my good intentions, I inevitably regret it. You cannot take back words once they leave your mouth, so think twice before saying something you'll regret.

My friend Julie is one of those rare creatures who pauses after you ask a question while she thinks of a proper response. I envy that trait and try to emulate it. If you are a 'blurter' like me, and say something inappropriate, apologize quickly so that hard feelings don't fester.

Leaders do not let their emotions control their words or behaviour. They take in what is happening, and respond calmly and confidently, always looking for win-win situations. Recently, after a day of very challenging meetings, a colleague said to me, "I admire how you kept your cool through that exchange, and stayed focused on positive outcomes."

While I may have felt strong emotions threatening to explode, I was able to lead others through an emotional minefield by staying calm.

Your reaction is your point of power

Positive results come from keeping your composure. I worked harder than ever, accepted my new boss, and was given a promotion to Associate Director. Had I cried, screamed or stalked off when they told me that I didn't get the job, that likely would not have happened. Quitting would not have punished them, just me and my family.

Emotions are normal, but don't let them control you. As author Michael Singer says, "Witness your emotion, and then let it go."

How often have you heard, 'They really know how to push my buttons!' It's not their fault that you have a huge button sitting out there for them to push. What is being triggered in you? If you journal, write it down. See how often that same button is pushed, and investigate why to prevent it from happening in the future.

My trigger comes back time-and-again to 'not good enough.' What story are you telling yourself? Not getting that job certainly pushed my buttons. By recognizing that pattern, I was able to stop the emotions in their tracks. Clear thinking unclouded by emotion allowed me to explore the real reason for the hire.

Be curious

> *"Curiosity only does one thing, and that is to give. And what it gives you are clues on the incredible scavenger hunt of your life." Elizabeth Gilbert*

When we take our eyes off ourselves, we are able to ask what other factors may be at play. Why did the other person make that decision or say those things? Be curious. What pressures might they be under, at work or in life? It's not always about you—give them the benefit of the doubt. In the case of the hiring, I'm sure our president was under extreme pressure to raise funds in the midst of a major recession.

Hearing that the successful candidate was on a team that raised a $25 million gift for another charity would have definitely influenced his decision.

Take a minute and write down the other person's perspective, point of view or pressure. Can you feel compassion or empathy for them at all?

Also be curious about how you might have contributed to any situation. As author Elizabeth Gilbert says, look for the clues in the scavenger hunt of your life.

Be confident

> *"Optimism is the faith that leads to achievement. Nothing can be done without hope and confidence." Helen Keller*

When you are able to deal with your personal triggers and put the emotions of a situation behind you, you will have faith that you can survive and thrive in any situation. It often helps to have a role model or mentor to lead the way and offer clues to success.

We seldom improve when we have no one else to model ourselves after. Who is your role model in business? What would the most confident woman you know do?

One of my role models is my book partner, Co-founder of *Success University for Women*™, Jan Fraser. As the seventh out of eight children, I learned early to unleash my razor-sharp tongue quickly. Sarcasm and humour were my weapons of choice, something I've been trying to tame for many years. Jan is the opposite—she never has a harsh word. While she may think it, she rarely speaks or writes it. Whenever I'm in a prickly situation, I think of how to 'Janify' it!

Courageously communicate your needs

> *"A lot of people are afraid to say what they want. That's why they don't get what they want."* Madonna

Speaking your mind clearly, confidently and tactfully takes courage. It's much easier to shrink than to ask for what you need. However, things will rarely improve without you speaking up. Difficult conversations can be risky. There is a certain safety in hiding your true self—no one can reject you if they don't actually know you. However, as Brené Brown says, "Vulnerability is the door to connection." Willingness to courageously communicate what you need will often lead to improvement in your situation.

> *"Courage is like a muscle. We strengthen it by use."* Ruth Gordon

I once had a boss who regularly rewrote everything I wrote, wordsmithing it to her own voice without changing the meaning. As a three-time best-selling author, that definitely pushed my buttons. I felt incompetent and like a bad writer. When I finally had the difficult conversation with her, she stopped herself and changed our work dynamic for the better. When have YOU been courageous in the past? If you were courageous then, could you be courageous enough to deal with this situation now?

Comedy: don't forget to laugh!

I don't believe in 'bad days.' I'm not about to give my entire day to a few 'difficult moments.' However, some days are easier than others, and sometimes you just need a good laugh or you will cry.

I have a 'Joy List' on my phone that contains things that fill me with joy or make me laugh. Write down 10 things that make you laugh, that can help you get through difficult moments.

Grace under fire

> *"The people who are lifting the world onward and upward are those who encourage more than they criticize."* Elizabeth Harrison

Tomorrow is another day. Handle each situation with grace and others will notice. If you don't handle it with grace, they will notice that, too. They may not remember the situation but they will remember how you handled it.

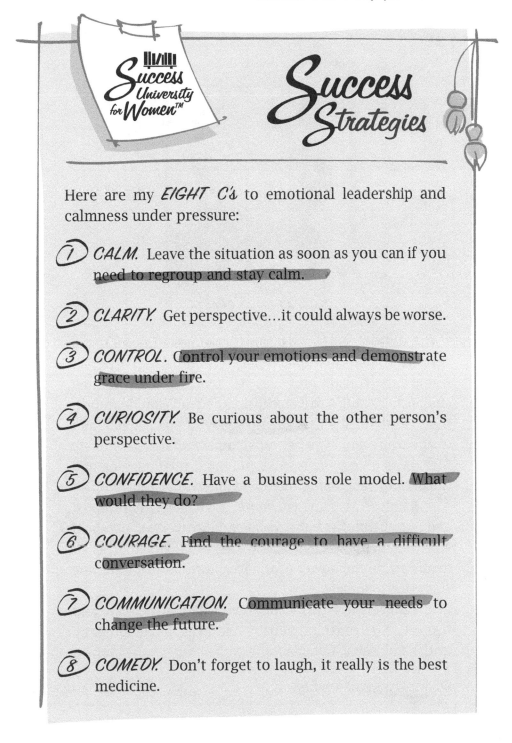

Success Strategies

Here are my *EIGHT C's* to emotional leadership and calmness under pressure:

1. *CALM.* Leave the situation as soon as you can if you need to regroup and stay calm.

2. *CLARITY.* Get perspective…it could always be worse.

3. *CONTROL.* Control your emotions and demonstrate grace under fire.

4. *CURIOSITY.* Be curious about the other person's perspective.

5. *CONFIDENCE.* Have a business role model. What would they do?

6. *COURAGE.* Find the courage to have a difficult conversation.

7. *COMMUNICATION.* Communicate your needs to change the future.

8. *COMEDY.* Don't forget to laugh, it really is the best medicine.

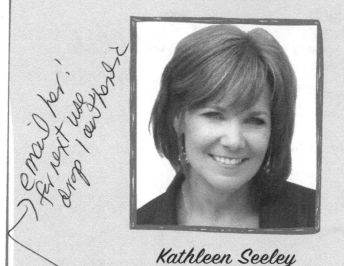

email her!
for next use
drop 1 question

Kathleen Seeley

Kathleen Seeley is an acclaimed international speaker, transformational coach, facilitator and corporate leadership consultant. She is focused on building sustainable, values-driven cultures and developing values-based leaders. She is authentic, edgy, walks her talk and unapologetically lives her most authentic and passionate life. She is able to gain trust and build relationships in a remarkably fast and authentic manner.

Kathleen is an engaging, articulate, humorous, and insightful Keynote Speaker. She weaves personal stories of her good and not-so-good moments in order to demonstrate the power of the transformational tools she shares with audiences.

Kathleen has three children, a daughter-in-law and two cats. She consults globally and lives in Salmon Arm, British Columbia, Canada.

www.massivelyhuman.com

SECTION ONE: CHAPTER TWO

Empowered Choices

by Kathleen Seeley

> *"I have learned as long as I hold fast to my beliefs and values—and follow my own moral compass—then the only expectations I need to live up to are my own."* Michelle Obama

ere it was, right in front of me, the gig of a lifetime. A man approached me after I gave a talk at a conference. He was a career politician, a successful businessman, connected and funded. He said my style and message captivated him, and he wanted us to build leadership capacity in his country. We were in alignment to develop values-based leadership on a global scale.

This could be it, my break! No sooner had we made our plans to meet, 'it' started. I joined him for dinner. The conversation was rich and I was present. I was captivated and on the verge of my long-held vision. I was so clear, excited and ready.

Then he made a comment. A hint. Of what, I wasn't sure. I ignored it.

Dinner ended and we made a plan for the next day. Then, another suggestion; I should switch to his hotel. I could no longer ignore my intuition, or could I? As I struggled to keep my head above the stormy waters of my thoughts, I remembered that the centre of all power is located in the awareness of why you make the choices you do, not so much in the choices themselves.

Trust your intuition

What do I do? What do I say?

I'm a strong, outspoken woman. This powerful man was holding my holy grail within reach. I told myself the suggestion to change hotels was to simplify our meeting the next day.

I brushed it off, but my intuition was screaming that something was off. It was at this moment I became present to my fight or flight instinct. I had to get out of there. "Refocus, ground yourself, Kathleen, you are overreacting. Get a grip!"

We arrived at my hotel, he walked me to the entrance, and then he said it: "I was hoping you would come and stay with me tonight." BAM! I could no longer deny what my intuition had been telling me. His intentions could not be clearer—he didn't see me as a collaborator, he saw me as a conquest.

Body shaking and heart pounding, my external response did not reveal what was happening inside. I hid my truth. Our inner-self is the best guide through a sticky situation. So I looked him straight in the eye and said, "I am not staying with you. I'll see you tomorrow."

I was a woman in the middle of a tornado and I was unwilling to acknowledge it was windy! How could I have been so stupid? I took the short cut to self-blame and negative self-talk. "It serves you right. Who were you to think you could play at such a level? It was never about bringing you into a project. You don't have what it takes. Stay small town. It's what you'll always be."

A haunting sense of self-betrayal set in. I felt foolish that I allowed possibility to seduce me. I visited a familiar place—self doubt. We've all been there; where we question, we doubt, and when we are shaken to our core, we sometimes forget who we are.

Notice, acknowledge and allow

> "Disturbance, confusion and a sense of chaos are not signs we are about to be destroyed. These are, in fact, the conditions which awaken us to our own possibility." Kathleen Seeley

I needed to find calm in the storm and win the struggle with my own self-destructive thoughts.

I took a breath and realized this state of mind was familiar. I became present to the moment, allowing it to be what it was. As quickly as the negative self-talk appeared, a new energy replaced it as I breathed, became present, and allowed it. I remembered who I was and I softened my heart. I wanted so much for this to be about him. I realized, in that moment, it had nothing to do with him. This was about me—about my values and boundaries.

Clear values create clear boundaries

As leaders, we face moments that call us to act from the parts of ourselves we have not yet occupied; those moments define us. I was facing a choice: I could make him the villain and me the victim; I could play along and flirt my way far enough to get what I wanted, or I could live my values and be clear about my boundaries, fully aware that I risked losing this opportunity. It hit me how difficult and disturbing living up to my values could be.

Living your values can push against comfort zones, loyalties, habits and beliefs. As disturbing as this can be, values pull us to hold ourselves accountable to the best possible version of ourselves.

I have spent years discovering who I am and knowing with certainty that while I do care about what others think of me, I care more about what I think of me. At the end of the day, I must face myself, a far worse critic than anyone has ever been.

Explore all options

Pure, empowered choice comes only when you consider all options, even if those options play out in the imagination. I realized I was confronting a conflict of values, nothing more. I could make him the enemy, but then I would deny what I know to be true: We can always find connection when we look to values we hold in common.

At every decision point, we face a choice to limit ourselves with the habit of beliefs or let our values pull us forward. It's not easy to live up to a value when so much is at stake.

No one is one thing

"You stand alone on your one square foot of earth—nobody else can. The implication of this can be as profound as standing up for your deepest values, or can be as simple as having the courage to say you are cold when everybody else appears comfortable." Ron Short

Third of Emmahnel - he has values and boundaries

Our values create boundaries—demarcating lines we will not cross. Our ability to articulate our values to ourselves and to others naturally results in clear boundaries.

If, in my own situation, I could not find a way to see our connection, then how could I affect leadership on a global scale? How could I execute my vision if I could not navigate this situation?

My ability to recognize my own process gave me clarity on who I am and who I want to be, both in this situation and in the future. My choices are empowered. My boundaries are clear. My actions are sourced from my values.

My reflection enhanced my ability to see him beyond the part that had triggered me; my world expanded, as did the realm of possibility. He was not the villain. I was not a victim. It was simple yet complex.

I chose to express what was true for me. I was nervous, clear and willing to walk away. With clear boundaries set and collaboration as my guiding intention, the project remains on the table. My vision to co-create leadership programs on a global scale is very much alive and possible.

This experience has been liberating and has led me to further examine my leadership. I could file the scenario as unique and completed; however, I know too much about myself to allow this to pass by without deeper reflection.

The difficult side of leadership is owning those parts of ourselves that are less than fabulous. I speak of those facets that, were they to be revealed, may risk our positions and reputations. No one is one thing. I am not, he is not, and you are not.

These are the places I go, in my own mind, and ask myself this difficult question, "Where else does this show up in my life?" How willing are you to look at the times you put yourself last? It is a difficult query. Our values can serve as touch points, a baseline measurement for when we leave pieces of ourselves behind or cause others to do the same.

Values provide personal clarity

Leading from values extends beyond the workplace and into our personal lives. Our values help us define our boundaries and I learned this from one of my children.

Not so long ago, my teenage son began to experiment heavily with drugs. He started smoking pot and that soon turned into using much harder drugs. As you can well imagine, this contributed to a great deal of conflict in my home. Creating a stable home environment for my youngest became my highest value.

There came a time that the conflict escalated to such a degree I could no longer have him in my home. I arranged for him to live with his brother and sister-in-law in another province. I packed his stuff and moved him without telling anyone. This caused tremendous conflict between me and my ex-husband. We both saw the situation very differently. Although I received a lot of criticism and judgment from people who only saw part of the picture, I knew I was doing the right thing for his safety and to create more calm in my home for my daughter. I spent nearly two years in the court system, enduring multiple hearings, preparing multiple affidavits, all emotionally draining and time consuming, to ensure he could stay where I located him and secure the financial support he needed to get well.

I was driven by my commitment to my values of family and safety. There was a time when my son was not allowed in my home. Previous visits resulted in him connecting with old friends and old habits soon followed. I was not willing to have this in my home with my daughter, who was then 12 years old. Although it was difficult to enforce this boundary, I knew it was the right thing to do. It was hard because he was hurt and angry but I was not willing to allow repeated behaviour.

I never wavered.

I am grateful to say he is now happy, healthy, has a full-time job and is welcome to visit my home anytime. He also knows I will not compromise my boundaries, should he relapse into past behaviour. I am proud of him. When we are clear on our values, even in challenging times, they help us through the most difficult circumstances.

Have I been in situations in which I compromised my values? Yes, most certainly—sometimes without awareness and other times by choice.

The centre of your power is located in the awareness of why you make the choices you do, not so much in the choices themselves.

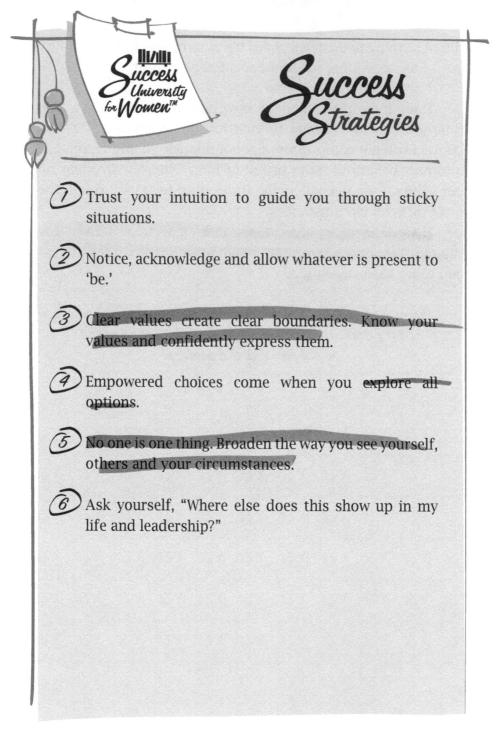

Success University for Women™

Success Strategies

1. Trust your intuition to guide you through sticky situations.

2. Notice, acknowledge and allow whatever is present to 'be.'

3. Clear values create clear boundaries. Know your values and confidently express them.

4. Empowered choices come when you explore all options.

5. No one is one thing. Broaden the way you see yourself, others and your circumstances.

6. Ask yourself, "Where else does this show up in my life and leadership?"

Notes

— Sense my intuition. Less so
now, but I have had the same
inner conflicts with men that
she described.

Dina Blanco-Ioannou

Educator – Coach – Teacher – Trainer

Founder of Lessons-in-Self, Dina is a professional English as a Second or Other Language Teacher, Teacher Educator, and Trainer with over 21 years of experience. She personally trained with Jack Canfield and is Certified in the *Success Principles*™ and the Jack Canfield Methodology.

Dina is an experienced trainer, having led workshops and seminars in Switzerland and at international teachers' conferences, women's groups and schools.

She inspires women and young people to authentically, meaningfully and purposefully realise their potential. Through her own life experiences, she shows no matter your educational background, culture and gender the life you rightly deserve is yours.

www.Lessons-in-Self.com

SECTION ONE: CHAPTER THREE

Free Your Inner Leader

by Dina Blanco-Ioannou

> *"If your actions create a legacy that inspires others to dream more, learn more, do more and become more, then, you are an excellent leader."* Dolly Parton

*T*he rebel inside me stirred. It was time to live the life I wanted. It was time to cause waves. It was time to step up, speak up, or fade away. "I want more! I'm here to do more!" I screamed at my father. He had just asked me why I wanted a divorce.

I wanted a divorce because I exercised for three hours at a time, six days a week. I harmed myself. I looked for acknowledgement and self-worth in affairs and one-night stands and gorged myself on food, vomiting until I felt empty. I wanted to pursue my dreams, go to university, study and become a teacher. I was a rare, English Greek-Cypriot woman who had the guts to break the rules.

I got married at 21. Partly because I believed it would make me the model daughter my parents desperately wanted. I would finally get rid of 'Dina, the black sheep of the family.' Now, my parents warned, in good 'ole Greek-Cypriot tradition, that my divorce would kill my mother and make my father so ashamed he'd never be able to leave the house. If I wanted that, I should "go ahead, and get a divorce." In those days, nothing was worth more than family honour...not even happiness.

Despite my family, I finally listened to my inner voice. My self-destructive habits had only made it louder, and there was no choice but to listen. It told me: "Trust yourself. Have the courage to make that decision, the one you've been putting off." I've found the most uncomfortable decisions create the biggest waves, and the biggest crash on our lives and transformational growth.

Freeing your inner leader starts when you decide to take control of your life. Make the decision to lead yourself with conviction and strive toward your goals.

Believe you will succeed, and you will.

Believe in yourself

> *"You must choose to believe you can do anything you set your mind to—anything at all—because, in fact, you can." Jack Canfield*

When we awake to our potential, we cause major waves, or even tsunamis, as I discovered. We create tsunamis when we choose to break free from the false perceptions and beliefs others have wrongly instilled in us. False beliefs have created the habits and thoughts we have about who we are...and are not. Take a moment to consider these questions:

What do you believe about yourself?

Where does this belief comes from?

Is it true?

Why do you believe it?

What do you believe is possible for you?

We accept most beliefs when our family passes them from generation to generation, rarely questioning where they come from. These beliefs include the expectations of us as women, our roles, our place in society and what we can or can't do. We accept them as part of our culture, and often follow and conform, and ask no questions; unless you are brave enough to start questioning these long-held beliefs and traditions.

For a long time, I felt as if someone was holding me underwater. Suddenly, with all my strength, I pushed myself up and took my first breath of liberating air. I finally broke the cycle. Everything in my life had a new sense of meaning and purpose. My world really was mine. I believed I could be and do anything I set my mind to because I could finally breathe on my own.

With this new sense of freedom, you start to believe in yourself and your potential. When you have determination, the right attitude and a renewed sense of self-belief, you are well on your way to accomplishing everything you set your mind to do.

The stronger your sense of self-belief, the more likely you are to succeed. Have courage to disregard beliefs that limit you.

Believe in yourself, your capabilities, achievements and all that you are destined to become.

Let faith lead you

"Faith is taking the first step even when you don't see the whole staircase." Martin Luther King

When my marriage ended, I left Cyprus and returned to my hometown of London, England. In the space of two weeks, I found a job as a Personal Assistant and a place to live. I wanted to go to university, but had no formal qualifications. This was minor, considering what I went through to reach this point. It didn't discourage me at all. I strongly believed and had faith that I would study no matter what; it was only a question of time.

Sure enough, it happened!

I was reading the local newspaper and saw an advertisement for exactly what I was looking for—a Teaching English as a Foreign Language (TEFL) teacher-training course. Amazingly, the course was at a school within walking distance of my office. By the end of the 12-week course, I qualified as a TEFL teacher with 'distinction.'

This experience showed me the important role faith can play in your life. Faith, in your higher self or the Universe or God, is always working in your favour and bringing your dreams to fruition. If you believe and feel as though you have already accomplished your goal, and attach a strong emotion to your intention, you will attract it to your physical reality. Don't worry about the destination and how to get there. As long as you are on the right path, are receptive and responsive to opportunities that arise, you are one step closer to realising your dream.

Having faith won't keep you from falling along the way, you will. It's how you get up again, brush yourself off and continue on your journey that matters. Believe you can achieve anything you decide, especially when you're unclear and wonder to yourself, "What now?" Have faith and let it lead you. In fact, enjoy the journey and everything you learn along the way. Remember faith knows where to go, trust it.

Keep learning

> *"Leaders are readers."* Jack Canfield

Never stop learning. Always be curious about the world around you. Work to be the best version of yourself, so when the opportunity you have been waiting for comes along, you will be ready.

Develop the skills and knowledge required to propel you onward and upward. Wholeheartedly embrace what you don't know, instead of allowing it to worry you. See opportunities for growth rather than limitations.

Since childhood, I've had a huge appetite for knowledge and a deep curiosity to learn. After my TEFL qualification, I discovered how much there was still to learn about teaching English. I read and learned everything I could about it so when the right university course came along I would be ready... and I was.

I believe reading liberates and enriches our soul and mind. It expands and nurtures us on our journey so success can blossom at the right moment. Make a list of topics you are passionate about and that inspire and interest you. Choose topics that are essential for your growth and success and start reading.

Commit to reading at least one new book a month. The more you read and learn, the more you become open and receptive to the amazing possibilities and opportunities the universe has in store for you.

Have strength

> *"I believe in being strong when everything seems to be going wrong." Audrey Hepburn*

Regardless of our path, life presents us with unwanted and unexpected obstacles. I think this is how God, or the Universe, checks in with us to see how strongly committed and passionate we are about our goals. Do you choose to fall at the first hurdle or find solutions, continue your journey with determination and finish the race no matter what?

This depends on the unshakeable foundation you build for yourself. When you have a strong sense of self-belief and faith, you will have the strength to overcome life's challenges.

If you find yourself faltering, do what I do, and take a moment to remember. Remember that life-changing decision you made...the one that changed the course of your life? Remember what you went through to get to where you are now.

If you can overcome those obstacles,
trust you can (and will) overcome
what you are facing now.

Acknowledge yourself

You are proof of how far you have come on your journey. Congratulate and acknowledge yourself for your accomplishments. When you acknowledge yourself and all your achievements, no matter how big or small, you will attract more wonderful elements into your life.

I am grateful for the phases of my life because I have learned so much in the process. I learned all women, irrespective of education and cultural background, are born with the capacity to lead. To lead others requires that we learn how to lead ourselves first. We need courage to embrace the essence of who we are, to be able to acknowledge and express our own needs, wants and desires. For many of us, to become the leader we were born to be we need to shatter long-held beliefs about what we can or can't do as women.

Freeing our inner leader requires belief, patience, faith, wisdom, strength and courage. Once free, we have the grace and capacity to authentically lead.

It's time to free your inner leader.

Success University for Women™

Success Strategies

1 Listen to your inner voice to lead and support you in making the right decisions.

2 Self-belief is the essence of who you are and who you are destined to be.

3 Let faith lead you because it knows exactly where you're heading, all you need to do is trust.

4 Continue to learn so you can grow and flourish. You will be ready when opportunity knocks.

5 Gather strength from your unshakeable foundation to help you overcome any obstacle.

6 Acknowledge yourself and all your achievements. You will attract more positive experiences into your life.

Tracy Quinn

Tracy is a global trainer, speaker, strategist, and leadership success coach. She is passionate about teaching entrepreneurs and corporate leaders how to achieve their personal, professional, and financial goals through her experiential teaching methods, enthusiasm, positive outlook, and ability to make real connections. Through value-based leadership programs, transformational coaching, experiential workshops, strategy retreats and mastermind programs, Tracy helps clients drive outstanding performance, strategic excellence, employee engagement and cultural transformation.

Tracy is a Jack Canfield *Success Principles*™ Trainer, Certified Barrett Consultant, and LEAN Sigma Master Black Belt. She has been leading technology and business transformations for global organizations for more than two decades.

www.QTessential.com

SECTION ONE: CHAPTER FOUR

Identify Your Passion

by Tracy Quinn

> *"Success isn't about how much money you make; it's about the difference you make in people's lives."* Michelle Obama

I was on the brink of burnout; emotionally drained, physically tired, and seriously stressed. My external conditions perfectly mirrored the degree of my internal discontent. I had spent my entire life chasing success, power, prestige, and the approval of others. I was living in a perpetual state of frustration.

I worked to get the best review, the next promotion, and more money. Success was defined by the number of zeros on my paycheck and the title on my business card. By those standards, I was successful. Considered a top performer, I was awarded extensive opportunities to learn, grow and travel the world. I worked with amazing people and had fabulous experiences. Others respected and depended on me.

Determination, commitment, and dedication had been my driving forces and had never let me down. Accomplishing whatever I set my mind to was easy. Without fear, I followed my intuition and acted without worrying about where it would lead. My confidence soared with each goal I achieved, encouraging me to continually set the bar higher.

Despite the toll of constant drive, I pushed harder. I wanted to create a more fulfilling lifestyle with balance, vitality, and wellbeing. More importantly, I desperately yearned to be engaged in work that would enhance people's quality of life, and use my time and talents in a way that fulfilled a much higher purpose.

Respect Your Values

> *"It's not hard to make decisions once you know what your values are."* Roy E. Disney

More than two decades working in corporate America taught me that our culture is based on lack...we are never good enough, powerful enough, profitable enough, rich enough, safe enough or relevant enough. When we wake up, we first think about how we didn't get enough sleep. When our heads hit the pillow at night, we think about what more we could have done. We spend the hours in between working to be extraordinary.

Corporate mindsets have shifted to focus on profit often forgetting people make the difference. I witnessed firsthand how detrimental a company's focus on profit and productivity over people could be. When working as a corporate leader, our company was forced to cut the bottom 10 percent of the workforce each year to show positive financials. I had been through the process five times, and this year was no different.

My team survived four grueling years working 80+ hours a week in a toxic environment, enduring overwhelming stress to meet unrealistic expectations. Against all odds, we delivered. The team barely took a breath before I was asked to eliminate eight amazing people from my team. My heart sank.

In that moment, I realized my values were not aligned with the company's. I set my future into motion with one pivotal choice: I resigned and left corporate America for good.

Removing Roadblocks

> *"It's not what happens to you, but how you react to it that matters." Epictetus*

Knowing yourself and respecting your values is critically important. Consciously or not, fundamental beliefs govern the way we think and act which can prevent us from reaching our fullest potential. The better we know ourselves, the better equipped we are to make necessary changes and become a positive influence to others.

Why did it take so long to stand up for my truth? First, I had to understand my truth.

I grew up in a home filled with fear and pain; abuse started at a young age, and bullying shortly after. Clear messages were driven deep into my psyche: I am not important; I am not valuable; I am not lovable. My 7-year-old self ran the show for a long time, determined to keep those messages alive, sabotaging any chance at greatness.

From an early age, I took on roles to deal with a lack of self-acceptance. As the achiever, my survival depended on collecting undeniable evidence of worth. Becoming the over-indulger, I gave endlessly to avoid future rejections. To prevent disapproval, the perfectionist stepped in to ensure I always looked good. Each role spawned from my need to survive the big lie—I am unlovable.

I fully embraced the message I'd heard repeatedly on my road to self-discovery—change your story, change your life—and rewrote my story. It took time and dedication but learning to love and accept myself and become grateful for who I am and how to express my true self to others has empowered me to become a better leader.

We each face roadblocks on our leadership path. Thankfully, you can free yourself from limiting beliefs. Start with self-awareness. Understanding and motivation flourish when you are willing to risk total honesty with yourself, challenge old assumptions and beliefs and have the courage to make changes.

Do What You Were Born to Do

"Your life has purpose. Your story is important. Your dreams count. Your voice matters. You were born to make an impact." Anonymous

My son knew exactly why he was put on this earth before the age of nine—to share his love of cooking with the world. He followed his passion without question, publishing his first cookbook two years later. It has taken half a lifetime for me to fully understand why I'm here, and sadly, some people never know. It boils down to understanding what brings you joy.

Life's purpose is to be your best self. Find your unique gift and share it with others. The universe rewards us with opportunities for our greatness to shine when we appreciate what is meaningful in our lives. Your best self serves others by doing what you were born to do. Your confidence and inner strength will radiate and inspire those around you to be strong, dream big, and live their lives to the fullest. You'll become the leader they follow.

Passion Fuels Success

Some of life's greatest treasures are often hidden and become clear when we decide what we want, follow our intuition, and act.

Asking, "What do you want?" is a great way to bring clarity. This question is simple and incredibly powerful. Honestly asked and answered, it more fully opens our consciousness. Random thoughts become clear and specific because they are fueled by passion. Asking this question repeatedly can challenge us to dig deeper and reach the heart of our desires.

Now that you know WHAT you want, determine WHY you want it. What will it bring you? How will it make you feel? What experiences do you want and what gifts would you bring to the world? The answer to these questions will identify your passion and become a powerful reason to act. As a leader, understanding yourself and what sparks your passion will ultimately help those you lead.

You Don't Have to be Perfect to be Excellent

> *"Choose connection over perfection."*
> Dr. Julie Hanks

Authenticity builds confidence and trust—two of the most powerful forms of motivation and inspiration. Being authentic is the most effective way of relating to and working with others and getting results.

As leaders, we need to focus on living our truth and establishing trust.

Have you ever watched a well-respected leader forget her words in the middle of a speech and laugh at herself? Chances are, you felt more comfortable around her. Humanness, not perfection, is relatable.

I've spent most of my life being the person I thought others would like and respect. Being afraid of what people thought prevented me from living my truth. Stories I held in my subconscious mind drove my actions. Thankfully, my commitment to change my story was stronger than my commitment to hold onto old beliefs.

It takes courage to be who we really are, not who others think we should be. When you are present as the real you, you create the freedom of authenticity and pave the way to living your fullest potential. You are unique and a gift to this world. It is irrelevant to compare yourself to others; what you have to offer can never be duplicated.

Feedback is Your Greatest Gift

> "Sometimes you can't see yourself clearly until you see yourself through the eyes of others."
> Ellen DeGeneres

Acting on feedback is the biggest differentiator between those who rise and those who get stuck.

Feedback highlights blind spots that affect your reputation and career, and allows you to create new behaviors and outcomes. It goes beyond how well you perform against goals. Feedback uncovers how your colleagues feel about working with you, how they perceive your ability to handle stress, how you communicate and collaborate, and, yes, whether or not you are authentic.

Hearing what others think hasn't always been easy for me. It occasionally invokes feelings of self-doubt and discouragement. I choose to follow the advice of Kathleen Seeley, a dear friend and mentor. She recommends sitting in the fire of that emotion and saying, "Welcome, would you like some cake?" Next, asking yourself, "What is one thing I can do to move forward?" Learning to listen and let go of our ego gives us valuable insight and empowers us to make positive changes. Feedback provides greater awareness of actions that allow us to become stronger and better leaders.

Make a habit of soliciting feedback. Welcome it. You can only address issues you know are there. Pretending you never make mistakes doesn't make it true. Usually, if one person complains, 10 more feel the same. Bring issues to the forefront to create an opportunity to face them head on. You can only improve if you are willing to ask, listen and act.

Experience incredible joy by following your passion and sharing your unique gift with the world. You'll live a more energetic and fulfilled life while making a difference to humanity.

May your gift light the way for others.

Success for Women™

Success Strategies

1. *Respect your values.* Always follow your heart and never compromise.

2. *Remove roadblocks.* Learn what holds you back and face it.

3. *Do what you were born to do.* Focus clearly on what you want, believe you can achieve it, follow your joy, and share it with the world.

4. *Fuel success with passion.* Tap into others' inspiration for motivation and encouragement.

5. *You don't have to be perfect to be excellent.* Be human to be relatable.

6. *Feedback is your greatest gift.* Use feedback as the guide to your best self.

Natasha Ryan

Natasha Ryan has worked with billion-dollar corporations and small business entrepreneurs. Her experience in systems, design and leadership delivers unique strategic insight. As a corporate consultant, Natasha analyzes and identifies growth strategy, implementation, and leadership development. Through integrated data management systems, she has managed over $20 Billion USD.

Natasha hosts Business Development, Public Leadership, and *Success Principles*™ workshops. She is a Barrett Values Centre's Cultural Transformation Practitioner, as well as a Canfield Training Group Certified *Success Principles*™ and Methodology Trainer. Natasha was trained personally by America's #1 Success Coach, Jack Canfield.

www.nrdcreative.com

SECTION ONE: CHAPTER FIVE

Champion Yourself

by Natasha Ryan

> *"Character cannot be developed in ease and quiet. Only through experience of trial and suffering can the soul be strengthened, ambition inspired, and success achieved." Helen Keller*

When I was 13 years old, my dad and I hiked a challenging trail in Alaska. A few hours in, my teen sass spilled out, "How long is this hike?!" "We are almost there. You're doing a great job, we got this," I heard my dad say as we came around the bend and out of the trees.

Ahead was a sheer-faced cliff. "We got this," my dad assured. Determined, we scrambled intensely to the top. We struggled, clawed our fingertips into the rocks, and pulled ourselves victoriously to the summit. I regained my breath, found my balance and turned to relish in the glory.

That moment lasted just a few seconds before I looked down. A wave of fear washed over as I realized I had to crawl back down. My father was still celebrating the achievement when he declared, "This is awesome, great work!" When he turned, he noticed my wide eyes, still body, and the odd silence of a teenage daughter.

He quickly shared a story about a Grand Canyon road trip when I was just a toddler. At a roadside turn-off, he heard shrieks and screams behind him. As he turned his head, he saw me fearlessly running toward the cliff. He sprinted after me. A full-bodied tackle nearly saved my life. Then, I cried. He picked me up, walked me to the edge, and held me far enough out that I would be too scared to ever run toward a cliff again.

As I listened to his story, I switched from gratitude to shock. Had the experience years ago shaped my present-day fear of this cliff?

As we live life, we collect stories. We are then built by the stories we remember, and those we don't. A story can take over the mind, and manifest feelings, emotions and reactions.

As a teen, I not only learned through trial-and-error how to climb up a cliff, but how to scramble over the edge and face my fear as well. Looking at my victory, I heard me, a champion, cheering from inside out.

Find Your Inner Champion

> *A champion is someone who fights for a cause or purpose that helps themselves or others.*

Sometimes, you must fight against your history or fear, and advocate for who you want to become.

Our life experiences, along with our thoughts, create stories. Some people become defined by these stories, as though life has already been 'written,' with a predictable outcome and they have tried and failed.

Champions collect stories. They believe stories serve them, propelling them onward to success. They don't see their history as a 'cap,' they see it as proof they are capable of overcoming. Champions learn through their struggles and turn their stories into fuel.

Different results emerge when you, consider—you. To achieve different results, one must change how they behave, contribute, or respond. We can lose ourselves in 'if' thoughts: if circumstances were different, if the other person would cooperate, or if we won the lottery. Rather than getting lost in the retrospective 'if,' try looking for the perspective 'if'... like Sinatra, "If I can make it here, I'll make it anywhere." The lessons we learn are the lessons we likely need to improve our income, health, and happiness.

You have lived with you your entire life. You have seen yourself on your worst days, your sad days. You were there when that frog turned into a prince—and when the prince turned into a royal jerk. When the credit card, the boy and the client turned you down, you have always had front row seats to your own story.

To learn how to champion yourself, start with an inward search. Allow yourself to wonder and consider the added perspective of 'how.' How did I contribute? How can I handle that differently next time? How did that situation feed into another? How do I benefit from this feeling? How did that serve me? Challenge your fears and limiting thoughts and replace your doubts with belief. As you consider all the possibilities, remember that you are the one suffering and growing in this moment. No one and nothing can relieve you of this awareness and growth. Let it serve you; learn to champion yourself from within.

You are extraordinary, magnificent, and designed to champion. To fight fear and programmed beliefs, you must battle back with vengeance and courage.

Be a Championer

> *"People who need people, are the luckiest people in the world." Barbara Streisand*

Has anyone ever asked if you 'will' do something? The first-date request is exciting, "Will you accompany me for dinner?" Later down the road that may become, "Will you marry me?" Eek! One yes leads to another.

At work, people make friendly requests, "Will you grab that off the printer?" or, "Will you help train the new guy?" As you support others and develop your strengths, those 'will you' requests may become something extraordinary.

I was 25 when a 'will you please' changed my life. I was just getting the hang of things at my first fancy, professional job. I jumped in with both feet, always willing to pick up lunch for colleagues or run an errand. Invariably, I would get the chance to eat with people in the office, learning the ropes from them. People got to know me and began to trust me, which opened doors of opportunity.

With time, I was trusted with select access to some of the company's most confidential information. I was excited to help, yet the responsibility weighed on me when I found out that the results were subject to audit by the Security and Exchange Commission (SEC).

During a monthly meeting, I explained my understanding of the challenges within the current protocol. Then, I took a leap of faith, advising them to scrap the in-place protocol and accept my plan for a new program. My plan guaranteed accuracy for the flawless standards required by the SEC, created a new more efficient process, and simplified individual and department participation. I also asked them to help me champion the concept, along with a massive budget. This meant, I was asking them to trust that I could deliver.

A few months later, I developed and delivered a system that met every SEC standard, brought new insight and opportunity to the company, and helped others. In the end, the program tracked transactions totaling $20 billion. Which was phenomenal, since I had never developed anything like this before.

Incredible results materialized because I championed the concept and refused to let my story of being young get in the way. As I believed in the idea, they believed in me. They saw I was looking for a solution for our team. As I became their champion, they became mine.

You Are the Champion, My Friend

"It is not a lack of strength, not a lack of knowledge, but rather a lack of will." Vince Lombardi

Rock bottom has built far more champions than easy street. Champions believe in themselves when no one else does.

You have to wake up, eat breakfast and go to bed with yourself every day. I often ask myself, clients, friends and guests at my workshops, "Who's the boss around here!?"

You have to live with the choices you make. That cupcake was fun going down and packing 'em on was a breeze…Yet are you beating yourself up about the 'fat' picture? You want to shed those baked goods…then it's rally time. Let's go! New job? Car? House? It's all waiting for you.

Believe in you, be your best company, and your biggest supporter, a champion from within. Walk your walk, success is around the bend.

How to STOP, LOOK and LISTEN Your Way to Success

When your stories or obstacles threaten your drive, collect your stories and use them as the building blocks to strengthen faith in yourself and others.

STOP: When you notice hesitation, stop. Consider what is behind this thought or emotion. Be aware, and wonder 'what if.' 'What if' this feeling is there by design to serve you? Consider simply, if you got a call with tragic news and had to drop everything and tend to a loved one—would this fear stop you or get in the way? Would it matter at all? Tell the fear to leave. You can rise above it, live in spite of it and re-define what fear means to you. Next time you hesitate, stop. Give yourself a moment to regroup. Then jump up and go. Your dreams are waiting to come true and the world needs you.

LOOK: Look at yourself as a brilliant movie producer. You are the visionary and creator of the next scene in the story of your life. While you are in this moment, '*STOP*' and watch the scene play in your mind. Look at all the options and move forward without hesitation. This is the moment you decide what's next. Focus on your vision.

Go for it...there is no failure—only lessons.

LISTEN: Speak or sing aloud to yourself. I know, it sounds strange...and it will feel strange. But you speak to everyone else in this world...Aren't you worth your own time?

LISTEN Option 1: Tell yourself how incredible you are...You are magnificent! All the junk, hurt, and pain that has happened or is going on now...you are still alive. Remind yourself about the incredible work you have done, and how you have grown. To push out fear you must do the work. If it seems too much for you...then ease into it.

LISTEN Option 2: What is your favorite song? The one with the lyrics that touch your soul. The song that stirs memories or you wish someone would sing to you. Find a place where you can be completely alone, lay on a bed, sit in a chair and play that song. Listen to the lyrics and feel as free as you felt at five years old...or even 95.

> *You are the one in charge. You are the boss of you...*
> *you are your greatest asset.*

STOP, LOOK and *LISTEN* to yourself. You have done it before, you are breathing now and you will breathe again.

There are no shortcuts. If you want something to change, it's up to you. Once you have done the work, these lessons will build your foundation for success.

> *Believe in you. Success awaits.*

Learn to Rule Your World

While you are climbing mountains, building your business, and leading your family, take a moment to relax and reflect. Be present with yourself and your ideas. It's taken you a lifetime to get this far.

Look to your story, your dreams and let your life inspire you. This is a big world, and there is plenty of room for you.

Champion yourself, your ideas and those around you. The only one in your head is you. Know that you are incredibly awesome. Your ideas, lessons and success depend on that champion inside. Let's conquer fear and do this.

The world is waiting.

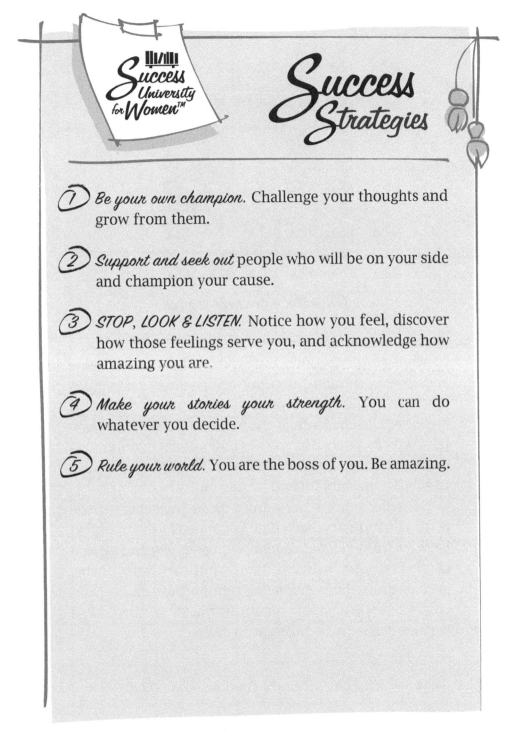

Success Strategies

1. *Be your own champion.* Challenge your thoughts and grow from them.

2. *Support and seek out* people who will be on your side and champion your cause.

3. *STOP, LOOK & LISTEN.* Notice how you feel, discover how those feelings serve you, and acknowledge how amazing you are.

4. *Make your stories your strength.* You can do whatever you decide.

5. *Rule your world.* You are the boss of you. Be amazing.

Giselle Commissiong

Giselle Commissiong is a passionate leader devoted to helping organizations, teams, and individuals navigate and break through barriers to positive change. A graduate of McGill University and Schulich School of Business, she has learned the power of purpose through her 20+ year career. Honing her obsession for continuous improvement as a business advisor, she focuses on ways to achieve meaningful and lasting outcomes.

Giselle started her career as an engineer in the aerospace industry, becoming fascinated by the interplay between individual motivation and organizational excellence. She believes that with the right focus, everyone has the potential to find purpose in life, and create a positive impact on our world. She is currently a Partner, Advisory Services, at EY.

www.linkedin.com/in/giselle-commissiong-20a499

SECTION ONE: CHAPTER SIX

Act Purposefully

Giselle Commissiong

> *"Even if you think you are done, you probably aren't, you always have a bit more."* Marnie McBean

*H*ave you ever known that you are about to make a significant mistake, and then made it anyway? Many years later, you realize that it was not a mistake, but the only way you could have learned an important lesson.

My 'mistake' was a personal one, made as a stubborn young woman, freshly graduated from university with an Engineering Degree and all the ingredients for a conventionally successful life: a dream career in the aerospace industry, devoted fiancé, new home, and plans for a grand wedding. I believed that these were the ingredients of a successful life, and here they were laid out for me, at such a young age! At least, that's the way I saw it. Why then, did it feel like I was heading into a trap? That's not quite the feeling you want on the eve of your wedding. Imagining this was just a natural part of the growth process and that I would eventually get over it, I forged ahead. The wedding was a blur and the very next day, I knew definitively I'd fallen into a trap entirely of my own making. I'd had the opportunity to avoid it and had done nothing about it.

What followed was the loneliest year of my life, full of introspection, isolation, and tears. At one point, I thought this was going to be my fate forever. However, in a rare moment of clarity, I understood that there was a choice that could only be made by one person.

The question was: what was the choice, would I have the courage to take it, and where would it lead?

Search for your purpose

Why was 'trap' the first word that came to mind? An objective observer might have called me ungrateful for what life had given me. However, I came to realize that aside from my career, I had not really made any hard life choices. I simply followed the path of least resistance and conflict all the way through and past the wedding.

Through a year of reflection, I came to realize that I didn't know what my life goals really were. I felt as if I had given up on purpose by being so lazy about the rest of my life. This was the root of my trap.

Be honest and own your decisions

My loneliness arose from the realization that I created this situation and chose, out of fear, not to act. I was afraid of disappointing friends and family, hurting my husband's feelings, and being personally embarrassed. I felt like a failure.

There were a few skeptics; people who knew me better than I knew myself at that point, but whom I ignored out of pride and the nagging fear that they may be right. In the end, I couldn't escape the reality of my actions. Honesty, with myself and others, would have served me well. Fortunately, it wasn't too late to change course, although it would certainly be more difficult.

Further years of reflection led to the mundane and obvious takeaway—I had been too young, inexperienced, immature, and stubborn to make such a big life decision at that point, without understanding the implications, and more importantly and especially, without seeking advice from those who offered it.

I learned the hard way—I had to own my past decisions, overcome my fear, and take action to reset my life.

Measure twice, cut once

While I spent the better part of a year mustering the courage to act, once that moment of courage appeared, I couldn't look back. Having decided to end my marriage and reset my life, I had to be ready for the consequences. I knew the reaction and pressure to reconsider would be overwhelming, and I was not disappointed!

My parents disapproved, his family was shocked, and I felt isolated from the people who were my bedrock. It was tempting to go back and make peace...but I knew wavering would prolong the agony, only to end back up in the same place.

We all feel the pressures of time. Sometimes, it makes sense to slow down and reconsider, but sometimes, moving forward decisively is the right move. Ripping off the proverbial 'Band-Aid' saved a lot of heartache over the long run.

Ask for help

Released from my 'trap,' I was unprepared for the deep feeling of loss that followed. Out of a sense of fairness to my ex, I literally left everything behind, signed away claim to the house and most of our belongings. I was determined to start again on my own. But I was still an immature, inexperienced, now 26-year old with a fledgling career, now living in a small one-bedroom basement apartment with a non-functioning stove. Around me, everyone seemed to have happily found their path. With a sense of having taken several steps backward, I had no clear picture of where to go next.

At work, I pursued more meaningful friendships with women with whom I had previously formed only superficial bonds. When I confided my struggles and sense of wandering, they were surprisingly supportive! I thought I'd be shunned and instead was embraced without judgement. Kristin, Kareen, Hayley, Lucinda, Liz: all became powerful supporters on my journey by sharing their own struggles. Through these women I learned the power of trust.

It would be difficult to ultimately make a difference for others if I was unable to share my own 'why' story. Be willing to ask for help.

Don't worry about being an Outlier

> *"Argue for your limitations, and sure enough, they're yours."* Richard Bach

Released from my trap, I could see clear path in front of me, although I didn't know its destination. The journey was uncomfortable, but I realized that was a natural consequence of change, and in the months that followed I grew used to it. Despite the skeptics, I was finding newfound peace with my decision. While it may have made me an outlier, it also made me more open to opportunities in other areas of life.

When I had the opportunity to take my first non-engineering role, a good number of my former colleagues found my decision foolhardy. Certainly a management role was not what attracted most engineers. However, by then, for the first time, not following the standard path felt right, and even exciting—although I still had no idea where it would lead next.

When opportunity knocks, answer the door!

Inspiration in unexpected places

"Ambitious goal setting, preparation, and action demand that you accept feeling both satisfied and unsatisfied, because no matter how much you do, there is always more that can be done, learned, or tried." Marnie McBean

Throughout my journey, one of my greatest sources of inspiration and learning was through sport, specifically rowing. I took up the sport as a novice, unexpectedly inspired by the success of the Canadian women's team at the 1992 Olympics.

All I could think was, "I want to be as good and as confident as they are." Although I was not destined to be an Olympic athlete, by understanding their world, there might be lessons I could apply in mine.

I made my first crew as the last selection in the women's eight, and set about learning as much as I could. Those early mornings on the lake taught discipline, teamwork, humility and resilience. I got used to being coached individually in front of others, for the good of the team, and became less self-conscious about making mistakes. I experienced deep disappointment when I didn't make the 'A' boat in the summer and was relegated to the 'B' crew, but made the best of it for the good of my new crewmates, finding new determination to improve and do better next time.

I was fortunate to have been coached by Marnie McBean for a few months. Her coaching tips always seemed to be equally applicable to life beyond rowing. "To go fast, slow things down in your head," she counselled as we were trying to increase our stroke rate. "Don't give people a reason to want to beat you," as we observed another crew making a show of how good they were. "Relaxing helps with balance," as we struggled to stay erect on a particularly windy day on the lake.

These invaluable lessons learned on the water have helped me to be a better person and leader.

Take care of yourself

Rowing is not only a source of life lessons, but also a revelation of the link between mental and physical health. The mental break provided by each training session gives me a respite from any worries on land, and teaches me to appreciate each moment rather than anticipating the one to come.

Having this mental break every day, this space for only me, provides a sense of purpose on days when I am otherwise uninspired. This self-care translates differently for different people: I have friends that meditate, play musical instruments, garden...even go sky-diving! Stepping away for a moment can provide a useful launching point for progress. In retrospect, that is what I did on a large scale for a year, and have now learned to do on a smaller scale. Any day that includes a vigorous workout is a good day!

Karma is Real

My heroes are not famous people; they are those who have taught me life lessons at critical junctures. An offhand comment from one of these people still sticks with me today, "You get back whatever you give out." Until this point, I had heard the word 'karma,' but did not understand what it meant. Like learning a new language, I had to practice...then one day I got it. Don't fight anger with anger, or fear with fear. There is nothing to be gained down that path. Bring others along with you, cheer them on, and find ways to lift them up. You learn as you teach. Be generous, even if others around you aren't. You often get back more than you give.

Purpose is a Journey

Now I know why I started this journey, years ago. It was not to get to a specific place, but to help others make positive changes despite difficulty. Most of our barriers are self-constructed, and can therefore be dismantled. However, it takes purposeful thinking and action, along with willingness to make calculated jumps into the unknown.

When we are armed with purpose and self-knowledge, we understand that our early life experiences are not necessarily destiny. Today, I am a successful businesswoman, respected by colleagues, and fulfilled in my career path. While ending my first marriage was the solution to get me on the path to purpose, marriage was not the root cause of my problem. I am blessed today to have found a new partner with whom I share complementary perspectives and goals. You can choose to change your path and determine your future.

The next chapter is still to be written.

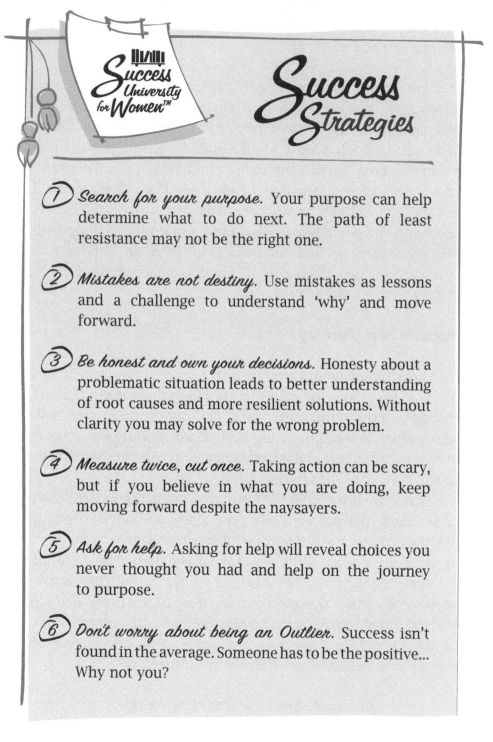

Success University for Women™

Success Strategies

1. *Search for your purpose.* Your purpose can help determine what to do next. The path of least resistance may not be the right one.

2. *Mistakes are not destiny.* Use mistakes as lessons and a challenge to understand 'why' and move forward.

3. *Be honest and own your decisions.* Honesty about a problematic situation leads to better understanding of root causes and more resilient solutions. Without clarity you may solve for the wrong problem.

4. *Measure twice, cut once.* Taking action can be scary, but if you believe in what you are doing, keep moving forward despite the naysayers.

5. *Ask for help.* Asking for help will reveal choices you never thought you had and help on the journey to purpose.

6. *Don't worry about being an Outlier.* Success isn't found in the average. Someone has to be the positive... Why not you?

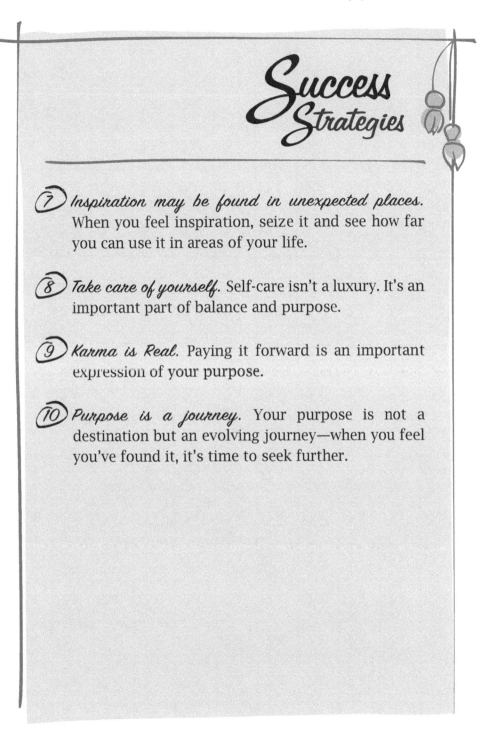

Success Strategies

⑦ *Inspiration may be found in unexpected places.* When you feel inspiration, seize it and see how far you can use it in areas of your life.

⑧ *Take care of yourself.* Self-care isn't a luxury. It's an important part of balance and purpose.

⑨ *Karma is Real.* Paying it forward is an important expression of your purpose.

⑩ *Purpose is a journey.* Your purpose is not a destination but an evolving journey—when you feel you've found it, it's time to seek further.

Section Two

Inspiring

SECTION TWO: INTRODUCTION

*W*hat does Leadership look like? We all know a leader when we see one—strong, confident, charismatic, knowledgeable, powerful, and hopefully compassionate. By their very nature, leaders inspire others to reach higher and do better.

Learn how the authors in this section became leaders, and how you can, too. They define leadership, live it in their daily lives and use their skills to lift others. *Lanette Pottle* of Maine tells us how she recovered from a destitute beginning to become a leader in her career. San Diego's *J.L. (Jani) Ashmore* shares the benefits of mentorship in her success path. *Diane Polnow* has been a sales leader for Fortune 100 companies who used her leadership experience to boomerang a low-performing team to the top ranks. *Bronwen Talley-Coffey* offers stories of inspirational leaders, and shows you how following their examples can bring success to your life.

Regardless of where you are in your career path, these chapters will inspire you to reach out and help others up, which is the true mark of a leader.

Lanette Pottle

Lanette Pottle is a success coach, trainer, and retreat leader best-known for her work helping ambitious women stress less and achieve more.

She is a past recipient of the Eleanor Roosevelt Positive Leadership Award, a graduate of Washington County Leadership Institute, and a mentor with Olympia Snowe Women's Leadership Institute.

Lanette hosts *The Success on Speed Dial Show*™, is creator of *The Time Creation Course*™, and is the founder of Rising Tide Network for Washington County Women In Business.

She walks her talk and lives her version of the 'good life' in small-town, Maine.

www.lanettepottle.com

SECTION TWO: CHAPTER ONE

Learn and Evolve

by Lanette Pottle

Katherine,
your willingness to lead
is creating a powerful, positive
impact in the world. Thank you!
♡ Lanette

> *"The secret of a leader lies in the tests she has faced over the course of her life and the habit of action she develops in meeting those tests."*
> *Gail Sheehy, author, journalist, lecturer*

At work for eight hours a day, I played a part. I acted. I stepped into the persona of the woman I wanted to be, with baggage and skeletons hidden well out of sight. By being the best at everything, no one would know or care about the fact that I'd been a single, teenage mom on welfare, evicted from two apartments and lived in a friend's basement with my toddler son. They wouldn't know I made poor financial choices and was hounded by bill collectors daily or that I had made a string of unhealthy relationship choices that put me in volatile situations. I created an alternate reality. I was living a double life.

I was an overachieving, people-pleasing perfectionist. I did what I was asked and was eager to take on more responsibility. I wanted to have the right answers to make myself valuable. I loved the recognition and headiness of being relied upon by others. I actively sought situations where I would be the smartest person in the room to be admired by others as a leader—but I was far from it. I couldn't lead my own life, and my insecurities rattled my ability to be a true leader for anyone else.

Through my twenties and into my thirties, I continued on this path. Gradually I began to realize that I couldn't fake my way to leadership. I started making healthier choices and investing in personal development. My situation improved and my confidence grew.

As I looked around at others I'd considered role models, I became aware that while they were good managers, they lacked true leadership abilities. With this shift in perspective, I began to actively look for women leading in authentic and inclusive ways.

New Role Models

Debbie was an exceptional leader. When I began working with her, I couldn't put my finger on the 'one thing' that made her different—made her an extraordinary leader—but she drew out the best in me. By example, she gave me a new understanding of what leadership could be. She was strong, had an infectious laugh, and seemed comfortable in her own skin. She was the type of leader who understood the importance of connection.

Debbie took the time to get to know me and what made me tick. She recognized my strengths and allowed me to incorporate them into my daily work, even when it fell outside the 'norms' of my role.

Debbie met my thirst for growth and knowledge with enthusiasm. She made it safe to show up authentically, even in moments we shared differing viewpoints. She invested time in building our relationship, learned what motivated me, and provided opportunities for me to be my best.

Her investment in me yielded what I consider to be some of my best work. I felt energized and validated in deeply meaningful ways, developing true confidence. She provided me, as Dale Carnegie said, "A fine reputation to live up to." Her positive impact carried beyond the four walls of the workplace, spilling over into our organization and out into the community.

It was in the community where I found another of my role models—Susan.

My relationship with Susan was not like the one with Debbie. I didn't know her personally or even work with her; I learned from afar. I watched her in the news and listened to what people in the community were saying. She intrigued me. Susan had gone from owning a medical billing practice to becoming the CEO of a broadband internet company.

She had many appealing qualities. What caught my attention most was her humility and acknowledgment of when she was not 'the expert.' She was willing to ask questions, then listen deeply to the answers. She fostered collaboration and connection as a pathway to providing solutions. She created an inclusive environment where people were invited in, felt heard and were appreciated.

The scope of this effort went beyond her business. Susan was a catalyst for bringing together mighty women from the community. She hosted monthly meetings so they could learn from—and support—one another. When attending one of these gatherings, I listened to a professional woman share openly about her history marked by significant personal challenge. It helped me realize there was power in my story.

Owning My Story

Sometime later, at a personal development event I attended, the facilitator asked participants to break into small groups and share a highlight reel of their life stories. It was uncomfortable but I didn't sugar coat anything. I was amazed how easily everyone opened up and how quickly our group bonded. Sharing was intensely powerful. At that moment, I knew that I would never hide my story again.

I don't share my story with every person I meet, but the important shift is that I am no longer afraid or ashamed of it. I understand that's who I am and recognize my story can add value. A leader isn't necessarily someone in a suit.

No matter what you've been through, you can develop skills and lead authentically from wherever you are.

True Leadership Creates Connection

Settling into my truth and letting my guard down made it easier to lead. I wasn't wasting energy worrying about being judged by others. I became more humble, kind, and compassionate. It softened my edges and improved my effectiveness.

In the workplace, my new perspective and approach helped me develop more trusting relationships. Delivering unpopular news and holding people accountable to follow policies is never easy but by leading with empathy, people feel valued in the process. Becoming skilled at asking meaningful questions provides useful insights. A sense of connection follows.

The commitment to lead with authenticity allows us to step more fully into our strengths and gifts. When our team sees us as relatable and approachable, they are more open to accepting feedback.

Work can be fun. We don't have to be stoic and serious to lead and achieve results.

The value of connection goes well beyond giving people a warm and fuzzy feeling. Connection uncovers ideas, deepens understanding, nurtures relationships, and builds trust.

Lead With Impact

As I approached my 40's, there was a message I felt compelled to share. I didn't set out to be a global leader, but my mentors, experiences and leadership lessons had prepared me for the next step.

Initially, I created a small online community as a place to uplift others through quotes and stories. I faced persistent challenges, including technical hurdles, living in a town of 500 people, and having a small personal network. However, my vision was greater than the hurdles and the community embraced my goal of creating a worldwide epidemic of positivity. Over 15,000 participants from over one hundred countries joined in and proudly carried the title of Positivity Ambassador.

Every person who became involved, created hope and excitement. I literally wept when a new member from South Africa joined our mission. Previously when the words 'epidemic' and 'South Africa' were discussed, the topic was HIV and its devastation. Now, the epidemic was positivity.

The mission of my organization grew to include action-oriented activities that brought kindness and positivity to the forefront. This included a grant program that recognized positive, purpose-filled youth who had ideas for doing good in their communities. One recipient, a 9-year-old girl was passionate about putting books into the hands of other children. Now entering high school, she remains a champion for literacy and leads with compassion and grace.

Being able to empower others and pass the torch of leadership is an incredible reward.

Regardless of our challenges, we can impact the world as we develop our leadership abilities.

The Evolution of a Leader

My journey is not unique. The path may look different but leadership always evolves. It has nothing to do with a title and everything to do with how we show up in the world—it's a way of life. There is always more to learn and new circumstances to challenge us. Leadership does not require perfection, only commitment. Wherever we are in our journey, whatever our background, we can become leaders in our families, communities, and at work.

Through leadership, we can influence powerful, positive change. We make a difference in our lives and the lives of others.

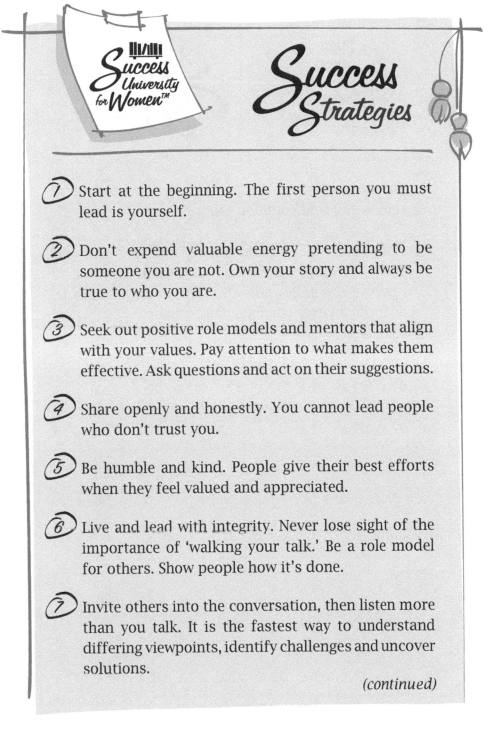

Success Strategies

1. Start at the beginning. The first person you must lead is yourself.

2. Don't expend valuable energy pretending to be someone you are not. Own your story and always be true to who you are.

3. Seek out positive role models and mentors that align with your values. Pay attention to what makes them effective. Ask questions and act on their suggestions.

4. Share openly and honestly. You cannot lead people who don't trust you.

5. Be humble and kind. People give their best efforts when they feel valued and appreciated.

6. Live and lead with integrity. Never lose sight of the importance of 'walking your talk.' Be a role model for others. Show people how it's done.

7. Invite others into the conversation, then listen more than you talk. It is the fastest way to understand differing viewpoints, identify challenges and uncover solutions.

(continued)

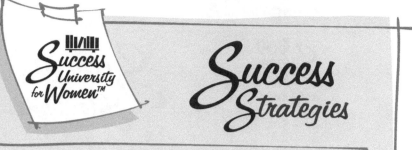

⑧ Show empathy and compassion. Meet people where they are to find common ground.

⑨ Keep an open mind and be prepared to evolve and grow. Recognize areas of opportunities; work to improve them. Be willing to try new approaches to adapt in an ever-changing landscape.

Notes

reminded me to - meet people where
they are.

- "own your story"-
- "the first person you must lead is
yourself."

J.L. (Jani) Ashmore

J.L. (Jani) Ashmore is an international Facilitator, Speaker, and Consultant to corporations in North America, Europe, and Asia Pacific. She helps executives to front-line employees in: Leadership, Sales, Customer Service, Communication/Presentation Skills and Team Building. Her dedication has contributed to 1,000's of people in 100's of organizations. Jani has been a trainer for such luminaries as Tony Robbins and Jack Canfield. She is President and a member of the Board of Directors for the non-profit organization *Global Family*. Jani has co-authored several Amazon.com™ best-selling books: *Success University for Women™ (Volume I); Success University for Women™ in Business (Volume II); Footsteps of the Fearless; Success Secrets;* and *Nothing But Net.* She has also authored *Stop Managing Start Inspiring: Keys for Leaders to Bring Out the Best in Others.*
www.janiashmore.com
janiashmore@gmail.com

SECTION TWO: CHAPTER TWO

Maximize Mentoring

by J.I. (Jani) Ashmore

> *"For every one of us that succeeds, it's because there's somebody there to show you the way...." Oprah Winfrey, TV Show Host, Motivational Speaker*

You never know when or where the perfect mentor will appear and change your life. It was springtime at La Casa de Maria in Santa Barbara, California. The vivid flowers were in full bloom, the skies were an azure blue, and the air was warm and breezy. I was pleased to be on retreat to spiritually contemplate and rejuvenate in the 200-year-old thick stone house that was previously a monastery.

It was six years after my 'calling' to ministry. I had not acted on the calling because I was confused. I could not see myself as a minister of a church with weekly sermons and handling other responsibilities. I sought council from other ministers. I was frustrated that I had not yet found my way to express that calling in the world.

Guests at La Casa de Maria spend the majority of their time in the solitude of meditation, contemplation, prayer, walking or reading. In contrast, guests eat the evening meal around a large family style table. One night fate sat me next to Saral Burdette, a lovely woman from Santa Barbara who regularly retreats to Casa.

As the first few minutes of any new conversation goes, I asked her about her life's work. She said she was a wedding officiant, a minister, who wrote and officiated wedding ceremonies for over 10 years. As she further spoke, every cell in my body lit up; I knew this was what I was to do with my own calling. I was elated at the prospect! When I shared my interest with Saral, she told me, "I can help you with that."

Saral became my mentor for the next three years as I learned the art, nuances, and business aspects of officiating weddings. She taught me to write ceremonies that are uniquely personal and meaningful to the couple, their family and the guests. I learned to officiate the ceremony with passion and heartfelt sincerity. Saral helped me get started by referring couples to me and specific guidelines of finding and attracting couples on my own. She did all this with compassion, passion, and encouragement.

As a result of Saral's effective mentoring, I am happy to say I have now been successfully officiating weddings for the last 12 years.

Mentors can guide our career, our work and how we live our lives. They can be teachers, family, friends or spiritual advisors. By mentoring others, leaders share the blessings they received in their life and career. It is an act of reciprocity, and the contribution to another can be immensely fulfilling and rewarding.

Mentor vs Coach

"A coach has some great questions for your answers.
A mentor has some great answers for your questions."
Anonymous

Throughout my career as a speaker, author, business consultant and wedding officiant, I have had many coaches and mentors. Saral was the perfect mentor for wedding officiating. Greats such as Tony Robbins, Patty Aubrey, Jack Canfield, Janet Atwood, and James Malinchak were the perfect mentors for writing, speaking and more.

A life or career coach is someone who may or may not have experience in your particular field. For example, if you are in a corporate environment, a coach may help you move to higher levels of management, but may not have the experience to help you solve industry related problems. A coach leans to the style of asking questions and helping you find the answers within yourself or encouraging you to find the resources for the answers.

A mentor is most helpful when she is successful and experienced in the field in which you aspire to succeed. They can show you the ropes and help you avoid the pitfalls. Mentors understand the strategies that work best in your field; they can open doors for you or introduce you to those who can further your career. Mentors can help you understand and traverse tricky company politics. If you are fortunate in life, you will have successful mentors, and be able to guide others in turn.

I was well into my career as a business consultant managing and leading workshops in a variety of topics, when the opportunity arose to share a subset of my skills. Angie was a colleague with whom I had enjoyed working for some time.

She was a sales coach and wanted to expand her skills to a higher position within the organization, managing workshops and mentoring coaches.

Angie was reluctant at first and uncertain she could do the job. I was delighted to mentor her through the learning process and help her find opportunities she had not seen before. After a few years, Angie grew to be one of the best workshop managers in her organization and remains so to this day. We were both thrilled with her progress. Through guiding Angie, and from my own mentors, I learned the skills of effective mentoring.

The Five Marks of the Mentor

> *"A mentor is someone whose hindsight can become your foresight." Anonymous*

Whether you are currently a leader wanting to mentor others, or you aspire to have someone mentor you, here are five markers of an excellent mentor:

Mark 1: Identifies Strengths and Areas for Improvement

A good mentor will help you identify both your strengths and areas you can improve. They can guide you in the technical aspects required for your job, and help you develop leadership skills. A good mentor will share her awareness of interpersonal skills, and help you explore your untapped potential. When seeking a mentor, look for someone who leads others by being the best at their job.

Throughout my career, I have mentored many training consultants. Each time, my clients complete a self-evaluation and we discuss the person's current skill level, where they aim to be, and any gap that needs to be filled to attain their goals.

Mark 2: Advises on Applying for New Jobs

Mentors are a terrific resource throughout your career, but especially when you are looking to obtain a different career opportunity. They may help you tailor your resume to the particular position and be willing to act as a reference for you. Role-play the interview with your mentor if their time permits in order to learn successful interview strategies.

As preparation for a job one of my mentees was seeking, we role-played interview questions she might encounter. We also worked together to ensure her resume highlighted skills and experience that shed the greatest light on her ability to do the job well.

Mark 3: Encourages and Affirms

Mentors can be your greatest cheerleaders. They should model a healthy, positive attitude, and be open and honest in their communication. Mentors encourage, motivate and affirm you as you move forward throughout your career.

While writing my first book on Leadership, I was fortunate to have Patty Aubrey, Co-author of several books in the **Chicken Soup for the Soul**® series as my mentor. Her encouragement and motivation were crucial in fostering my ability to complete and publish my own book.

Mark 4: Develops Strategies to Move Forward

Mentors can prove invaluable in advancing your career. From goal setting and accountability, to identifying resources and removing barriers for advancement, mentors can show you the way.

They can often open doors for you through networking and personal introductions.

One of my clients, Mark, a Regional Sales Manager, mentored an employee in his company. Mark not only helped him set goals and take action, but also held him accountable in reaching those goals. Mark's knowledge in the field and his help in developing strategies allowed the employee to make a major change in his career and become #1 in his company.

Mark 5: Shares Wisdom

One of the key aspects of being a mentor is the ability to transfer knowledge. As the saying goes, 'there is no sense getting older without getting wiser.' Mentors have been where you are, and can help you avoid the mistakes they made. Learn through their personal stories and experiences to successfully navigate your own path.

Identify someone ahead of you on your career path that can help you with specific skills. Ensure it is someone positive and compassionate who will offer feedback instead of harsh criticism. Ask them about your blind spot—we can't change what we don't see. They might help you identify incorrect assumptions, wasteful efforts or beliefs that are holding you back. Ask them for constructive feedback.

In my work with Jack Canfield, author of **Success Principles**™, his wisdom as an author, speaker and trainer was invaluable to me. His style of conveying strategies, identify limiting beliefs, and offering feedback helped me maintain my self-esteem and attain the next level in my career.

Jack's passion for helping others was infectious, and informed my career choices.

Leave a Mark or Allow Others to Leave One on You

> *"A leader can be anyone who steps forward and demonstrates effective ways of speaking, modeling, or motivating themselves and others to be the best that they can be."* J.L. (Jani) Ashmore

Leaders aren't merely those with the words 'manager,' 'executive,' or 'supervisor' in their title. You can show leadership by simply picking up a piece of trash as you walk down the street, or being first to volunteer on your team for an unassigned task.

Be a leader and a mentor by sharing the lessons you once received or learned through experience. Help others to become the best in their field, and feel fulfilled by their work. Be open to the advice and mentorship of others around you, and always remember what others have to teach.

If you do, your mentoring relationships can be deeply rewarding.

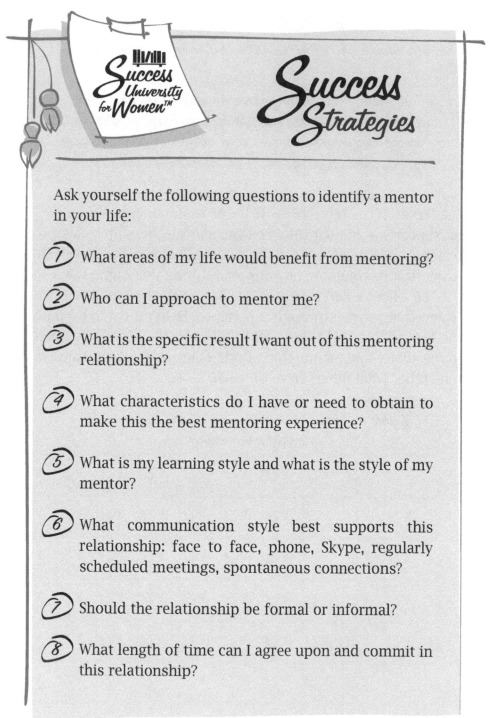

Success Strategies

Ask yourself the following questions to identify a mentor in your life:

1. What areas of my life would benefit from mentoring?

2. Who can I approach to mentor me?

3. What is the specific result I want out of this mentoring relationship?

4. What characteristics do I have or need to obtain to make this the best mentoring experience?

5. What is my learning style and what is the style of my mentor?

6. What communication style best supports this relationship: face to face, phone, Skype, regularly scheduled meetings, spontaneous connections?

7. Should the relationship be formal or informal?

8. What length of time can I agree upon and commit in this relationship?

Success Strategies

9) Is it necessary to create agreements and sign a written commitment?

10) What else will best prepare me for this mentoring relationship?

Diane Polnow

Diane Polnow is CEO of Elite Sales Leaders, a consulting and training firm that helps Sales Managers and Sales Executives drive peak sales results using her proven strategies.

Diane is an expert at driving sales results at some of the most recognizable Fortune 100 companies. She spent nearly 20 years with Sprint and American Express amassing numerous awards for top performance year after year. Diane was a consistent Top Performing Sales Leader at Sprint, achieved multiple President's Club Awards, and led some of her direct Account Managers to achieve President's Club Awards as well. Moving to American Express, Diane inherited a team ranked #33 in the nation and led them to #4.

www.elitesalesleaders.com

SECTION TWO: CHAPTER THREE

Rise to the Top

by Diane Polnow

> *"Difficult roads often lead to beautiful destinations."*
> *Anonymous*

F alling from the top to the bottom of the barrel knocked the wind out of me. I resigned from a 14-year career with one of the nation's top sales teams for one who ranked #33 of #34. I always strived to be elite in my field, so this was a huge challenge. As sadness, worry and stress took hold, self-doubt crept in. I didn't know the industry, people, product offers, processes and so much more. Would I ever get to the top again? The top represented security, which is extremely important to me.

From an early age, I had to support myself financially. My father passed away of a massive heart attack on-the-job, one month after his 50th birthday. I lost my mother six years later.

Money was my security and I did not want to worry about my financial health.

Thankfully, my big toolbox of proven success strategies helped me lead the team to #4 in the country. It wasn't easy, but it was worth it—and boy did it feel good.

Some of these proven success strategies will save you grief, heartache, stress, and energy. They've worked in every leadership role I have had, and they have made me a stronger leader. They will work for you too.

Embrace Change

> *"If you don't like something, change it. If you can't change it, change your attitude."* Maya Angelou

Become comfortable with the uncomfortable. Most of us are creatures of habit who like our comfort zone and resist change. Unfortunately, leadership requires constant change. We need to 'roll with the flow' for a more pleasant journey. For any company or person to be successful, they must adapt to change. I knew change was inevitable with this new position.

First, I had to look inside and figure out how to fit into this drastically different culture. Next, team changes were made; sometimes there are good people who aren't the right fit for the job. Finally, I helped others change behaviors that didn't work, and taught new ones that did.

Surviving multiple reorganizations, a company merger, and a multitude of changes in my career equipped me to embrace change in this job. When the company announced changes to policies, compensation, quotas, upper management, job titles, territories, accounts, and more, I calmly explained the why's and the benefits to my team. I reinforced that no matter what, everything would be okay. They could still dominate the top and make big bucks if they wanted to...and they did.

Find a Way

> *"If you really want something, you will find a way. If you don't, you'll find an excuse." Jim Rohn*

When you have a will, you will find a way. Always lead with the mindset that you work for your team, they don't work for you. I worked to remove or resolve roadblocks, challenges, and whatever would impede my team's success. The team rose closer to the top because I refused to take no for an answer. We were resourceful and looked for allies that said, "Yes, you can offer that. Yes, we will approve that."

I thought outside the box to make things work, and found ways to help them close deals, get new appointments, have difficult conversations, work through personal problems, and so much more. When you help others achieve their goals, you achieve yours.

Remove Emotions and Stick with the Facts

> *"No matter the situation, never let emotions overpower your intelligence." Anonymous*

Here is the truth: being in a leadership role can be highly emotional for both men and women. Become a Master of building cases filled with facts, not emotions.

When my team came to me with an emotional situation, I coached them to stick with the facts. It wasn't cold; when you hear the facts, it better equips you to make important decisions. Focusing on the facts makes you a leader that can easily find solutions to problems. Each time they managed their emotions, the team rose in the rankings and they reaffirmed this technique.

This approach can be especially powerful when you elevate issues to management and executive levels. Take no offense: most want the bottom line, not how you feel about it.

Choose Your Battles

> *Choosing the right battles is one thing. Choosing who you battle, and don't, is equally important. One without the other could be devastating to your ultimate outcome.*

People from all sides will want and expect things from you as a leader both up and down the organization. Save your energy. You can't and won't want to fight every battle. Learn early on when to fight for the cause and when to let go. Learn whom to battle. If you battle too aggressively, it could tarnish your brand and put you in a bad position.

I knew I couldn't fix everything, or be everything to everyone, so I mindfully chose which battles to fight. My team knew I had their backs, and I set proper expectations for when the outcome wasn't in their favor.

Important battles were those high-impact issues such as compensation, deals and integrity. I quickly learned who would help me and who would immediately say no. Find advocates and people who will partner with you, and then be sure to recognize and thank them.

Be in Integrity

I got to the top by doing the right thing and coaching my teams to do the same. There was an expectation to maintain integrity and always do the right thing—even when no one was looking. Credit was given where it was due, including to the support staff and other departments that were instrumental in our successes. I put my head down, did my job, and didn't boast about myself when we reached higher-performance levels.

At the end of the day, when you put your head on the pillow, you will know you've done the right thing—even if it's not the most popular.

Continue to Grow

In leadership, you don't have to do it alone. There are people who are highly skilled and sincerely want to help you succeed as a leader.

My role as a leader became easier and much more rewarding when I had a support system. It was invaluable for me to know that mentors, coaches, leaders and others could give me a needed sanity check. They helped me breakthrough, and gave me unbiased coaching and advice. I didn't depend on my boss to do this for me.

I believe school is always in session. I consistently invested in my own personal growth. Without question, it led to my professional success. The two are connected.

Strive for and expect excellence—from yourself and those you lead. You can achieve your goals when you stay committed to personal and professional growth.

Persevere and Keep It Fun

No matter what life throws at you, remember why you are a leader. Why do you get up every day and lead others? Is it for your family, financial health, or because you love it?

Take the role of leader seriously; it can change someone's financial future. You can help someone buy a home, save for early retirement, take a dream vacation, and more. You may be the one person who believes in them, recognizes them, and encourages them.

I admit that money is one of my why's. As I mentioned earlier, having lost my parents early in life, I have always had to support myself. I also persevere because my parents never got the opportunity. The moment I lost them taught me to live life while you can.

To me, financial freedom allows me to live a dream life. I've been blessed to earn and save money, live debt free, travel to 16 countries, live on the beach with a 180-degree ocean view and have a new family of fabulous friends and priceless memories. I've had a lot of fun along the way.

What's your why? Allow that to fuel and inspire you to persevere through the toughest times.

If you're going to be a leader, be elite.

Put your goals in front of you, decide what you're passionate about in this life, and find a way to make them happen. Don't let adversity, challenges, obstacles or others tell you that you can't. There are many beautiful destinations waiting for you.

Here's to your success as a leader!

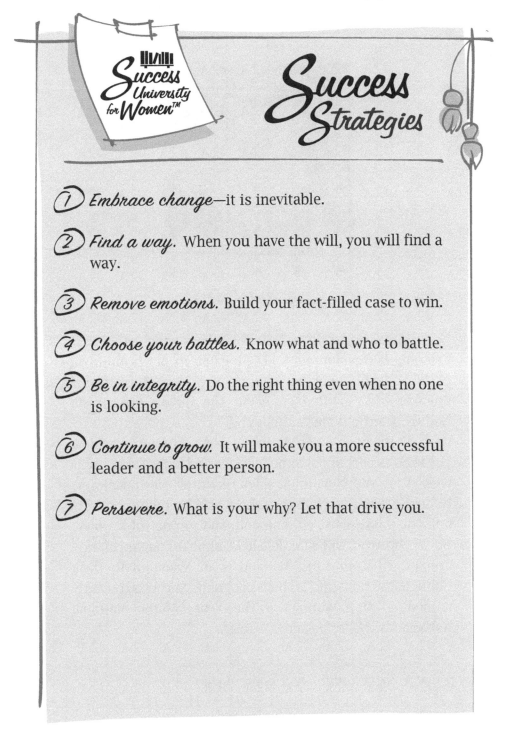

Success Strategies

① *Embrace change*—it is inevitable.

② *Find a way.* When you have the will, you will find a way.

③ *Remove emotions.* Build your fact-filled case to win.

④ *Choose your battles.* Know what and who to battle.

⑤ *Be in integrity.* Do the right thing even when no one is looking.

⑥ *Continue to grow.* It will make you a more successful leader and a better person.

⑦ *Persevere.* What is your why? Let that drive you.

Bronwen Talley-Coffey

Bronwen Talley-Coffey is the owner of Aspire Training & Development, LLC, located in her hometown of Waynesville, North Carolina. She is a Motivational Speaker and Certified Trainer in the *Success Principles*™ and the Canfield Methodology.

With over 30 years in sales and public relations, she is an expert in customer service and sales training, as well as an award-winning sales recruiter. Her passion is to create positive change in the world by helping others become passionate, enlightened, and impactful leaders.

Bronwen will complete her Cultural Transformation Tools Certification in 2017 and is an Assistant for Jack Canfield's Train the Trainer program. She was recently named a 2017 Woman of the Year by the National Association of Professional Women.

www.AspireTrainingDevelopment.com

SECTION TWO: CHAPTER FOUR

Motivate with Heart

by Bronwen Talley-Coffey

> *"I don't go by a rule book...I lead from the heart, not the head."* Diana, Princess of Wales

O ne of my first jobs was working in a male-dominated automotive dealership in the lowest-recognized position. As a receptionist, I was expected to simply answer the phones, write gas vouchers, and issue dealer plates for test drives. Even though I wasn't expected to do more, I've never been the type of person to complete only the bare minimum requirements of any endeavor. Being a dedicated employee, I was determined to hone my already impressive office skills and become a certified Administrative Assistant. While other receptionists before me had spent countless hours reading romance novels and gossiping about coworkers, I spent my time studying books, office manuals, and taking online tests. After several months, I earned my certificate.

I cared for those I worked with and I always tried to treat everyone, from the cleaning crew to the general manager, with respect. I made sure there was fresh-brewed coffee available throughout the day while keeping the reception area clean and the manager's offices organized. On occasion, I surprised fellow coworkers with breakfast items, doughnuts, or other goodies.

My refreshed and newfound administrative skills allowed me to write letters, conduct research for various managerial projects, and complete reports for upper management. I was known for going above and beyond my duties providing exceptional customer service. I stayed late to complete time-sensitive tasks, filled in for part-time receptionists who were unable to report to work in the evenings, and was just a phone call away if anyone had a question or needed assistance. My hard work paid off—I was awarded one of only two merit raises given that year.

Most importantly, I was best known for my personal attributes, such as bringing coworkers a birthday treat and acknowledging former soldiers on Veteran's Day with a card and catered lunch. These actions let others know that they were important and deserved to be recognized. In turn, I discovered I was respected and appreciated by many of my coworkers.

Be a Leader in Every Role

> *"Do not wait on a leader…look in the mirror, it's you!"*
> Katherine Miracle

Many years later, after speaking at a conference, I was approached by Jan Fraser, one of the founders of this book, a woman I highly respect and admire. I was surprised when she invited me to contribute a chapter on leadership. Honestly, I had never considered myself to be a leader. You may feel the same. Rest assured, you don't need leadership awards or a prestigious title to be a leader. As I began looking back, I realized that I had been playing the role of a leader, sometimes unknowingly, for most of my life. There are opportunities every day for seemingly ordinary people to step up and be great leaders.

In my youth, I was a dancer in every genre, from tap to ballet and pointe. One year, I participated in our annual dance recital with a cast up to my knee after I broke my foot during a dance exhibit. It never occurred to me to sit out, as I knew it would let the other members of my team down. The other girls recognized my grit and perseverance and named me the Most Valuable Member of our dance troupe. We can show our support for others and lead by example at any age, in any situation.

Later, as a wife and stay-at-home mother, I worked for myself in direct sales and network marketing while managing a household and raising a daughter. I showcased products easily and reached the top levels in different companies. That's when I learned that I could achieve my goals while supporting those I loved most. As a successful leader, it's important to remember that once you reach the top, it's your responsibility to share your path to success with others.

There was a time when I left the world of entrepreneurship to rejoin the workforce. As an employee, I felt like I was working to help someone else achieve their goals and make their dreams come true. Upper management took a lot of personal time and several paid vacations per year, while those below them were overworked and had few paid benefits. The work environment became toxic with resentment and disgust. After seeing how disheartened the employees in that workplace became, I was determined to make the atmosphere in my own business personable and uplifting. That was my start to becoming a transformational leader.

Look back at your own life and see what defining moments have shaped you into the person you are today. Sometimes, the events in our past that seem the worst are the ones that teach us the most. My experiences taught me many lessons, including how to make a difference in someone's life and help others persevere.

What have your life experiences
taught you about reaching beyond
yourself to lead others?

Follow Your Heart: It Knows the Way

When I think of strong female leaders, two recent examples come to mind. Both Princess Diana and Dolly Parton have shown strength and compassion for human kind. Their examples influenced me early on and helped shape the woman and leader I am today.

> *"I'd like to be a queen in people's hearts."*
> *Diana, Princess of Wales*

Princess Diana did not fit into the royal establishment because she did not follow their rules. Yet, she believed she had a role to fulfill. She spoke of people having become indifferent and not caring anymore and that people feeling unloved was a disease. She believed that giving love was like giving light in dark tunnels and spent her life in that pursuit.

Diana led with her heart. People overlooked her human faults because her leadership style was so compelling. Twenty years after her death, Diana's words and actions are still influential. Her legacy of good works lives on through her sons. Diana's memory encourages people around the world to put others before self, to volunteer, and to care. She got her wish—she did become the queen of the people's hearts.

> *"If your actions create a legacy that inspire others to dream more, learn more, do more and become more, then you are an excellent leader." Dolly Parton*

Dolly Parton is a country music icon, a Country Music Hall of Fame inductee, and the most honored female country performer of all time. She is also a successful business woman and philanthropist. She embodies true leadership.

She and I grew up in the same beautiful Great Smoky Mountains, a place we both still consider home. Her humble beginnings and strong faith are evident in the heartfelt contributions she continues to make to family, friends, neighbors, and society. She created Dollywood, a theme park in Pigeon Forge, Tennessee, ensuring her family members always had a place to work and provide for their families. Through the Dollywood Foundation, Dolly has supported many charitable efforts, particularly in the area of literacy. Her Imagination Library mails one book per month to each enrolled child, including my godchild, from the time of their birth until they enter kindergarten, with over 850,000 children from four different countries participating each month. Her efforts are not limited to mankind; she is highly regarded for her efforts to preserve America's symbol of freedom, the Bald Eagle, through the American Eagle Foundation's sanctuary at Dollywood.

The 2016 wildfires that swept through the Great Smoky Mountains in Pigeon Forge and Gatlinburg, Tennessee, also proved that Dolly is a strong leader. After the wildfires left 14 dead and hundreds displaced, she created the My People Fund, giving over 900 families $1,000 per month for six months. At the end of that time, there was enough left in the fund to give each family an additional $5,000. Contributing an additional $3M to the Mountain Tough Recovery Organization, she partnered with community leaders to address the longer-term needs of the residents affected by the fire, such as housing, employment, and counseling. Dolly uses her resources and follows her heart to lead by helping others.

Not all of us have the prestige or wealth to do what these incredible ladies have accomplished. The same way a non-profit organization has the capability to raise money for their cause, leaders find ways to achieve their goals by incorporating their own strengths with the strengths and connections of others.

By having a clear and precise vision, following your heart, and desiring to make a difference in the world, we can lead as these memorable women have done.

Uplift and Empower Others

I met Lauren, an assistant at my local veterinarian's office, a couple of years ago when she was pregnant with her first child. Needing additional income, she became a consultant with my former skincare business. After the birth of her daughter and some circumstances beyond her control, I offered Lauren a position as a receptionist with my newly-formed training and coaching business, Aspire Training & Development. Being a single parent, this afforded her more flexible hours and increased pay. She happily accepted and we began working together. As other employees came on, her workload increased and she was promoted to Office Manager, with a pay raise and benefits.

Understanding all too well how single parenthood could bring various challenges, I offered support and advice to Lauren anytime she asked for it, and financial assistance on occasion. When Lauren asked my opinion on applying for a home through Habitat for Humanity, I encouraged her to apply. A couple of months later, she received the news that she was qualified and a new home would be built for her and her daughter.

As part of the agreement, she was required to volunteer for 300 hours to acquire the home. With a full-time job and difficult living conditions, she became overwhelmed and depressed. Lauren received a call from a lady at Habitat asking for a meeting. When she got there, Lauren was informed of a surprise they had for her. A home that had been built several months prior was being vacated and since she was next on the list, she could opt to take it instead of waiting for her new house to be completed within the next year. Lauren was over the moon! However, without the volunteer hours completed, she would lose her chance to get into this home. That's when I knew what I had to do.

That August afternoon, I called Lauren into my office and told her that she would not be working for me at the office for the next month. Her panicked look said that she thought she was losing her job. I explained that throughout the month of September, she would be volunteering for Habitat for Humanity during the same hours she would normally work for me. That would give her between 32-40 hours per week to add to her volunteer hours she had already accumulated.

The catch? She would continue to get a pay check every week from my business even though she wasn't there. My two other employees offered to cover her office workload while she was out.

I also arranged for more than a dozen volunteers to show up one Saturday and put in hours that would count toward her

300 hours needed to receive her home. My goal was to get her and her child in that house before cold weather hit.

Not every business can do what our business did for Lauren. However, it is my belief that any small gift, not always monetary, goes a long way in creating quality employees. As we empower others, we show them what it means to lead.

Even though Lauren is a strong woman in her own right, the love and support she received from me, her coworkers, family, friends, and even strangers, made a world of difference in how she views the future. She feels the need to pay it forward and offers some of the same gifts to others that she received.

Businesses need to move beyond technological leadership (robotic) to transformational leadership (human). The key is understanding that the corporation is made up of humans. Treating one another within the corporation as an individual, getting to know those individual's values and goals, and allowing guidelines to be set forth with human needs and circumstances considered, we create a desirable environment for people to thrive. This creates a new dynamic where people feel valued and no longer see those they work with as competitors, but as collaborators and mentors. A stronger team of individuals creates a powerful corporation that makes a difference in the world. Therefore, the ultimate leadership goal should be to uplift and empower people in your presence and have them stay that way in your absence.

As Mother Teresa once said, "Do not wait for leaders; do it alone, person to person. Be faithful in small things because it is in them that your strength lies."

You have amazing strengths within yourself that you can apply to any aspect of your life, personally or professionally, no matter your role. Let your strengths shine through in everything you do, big or small, with everyone you meet.

Always make it your goal to lead from the heart, lifting and empowering people along your path.

Not only will you grow as a person, your example will lead others to do the same.

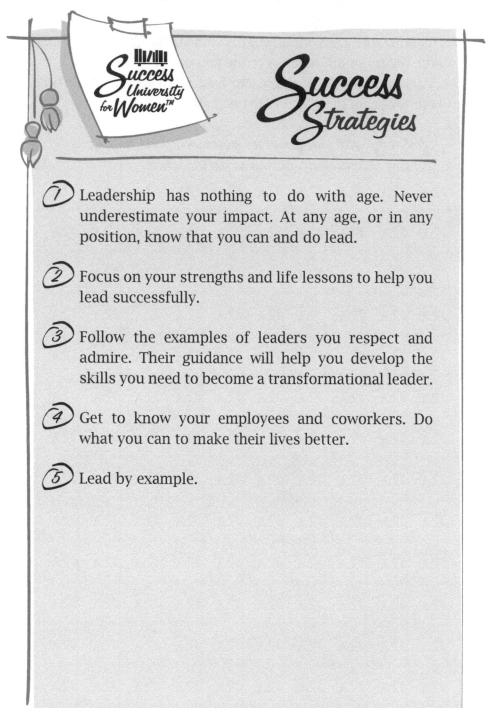

1. Leadership has nothing to do with age. Never underestimate your impact. At any age, or in any position, know that you can and do lead.

2. Focus on your strengths and life lessons to help you lead successfully.

3. Follow the examples of leaders you respect and admire. Their guidance will help you develop the skills you need to become a transformational leader.

4. Get to know your employees and coworkers. Do what you can to make their lives better.

5. Lead by example.

Notes

Section Three

Unifying

SECTION THREE: INTRODUCTION

You've likely heard the expression, "It takes teamwork to make the dream work." But what does it take to create the dream team? The authors in this section show how leadership, or a lack of it, can make or break a team. Learn from their stories how to successfully motivate your team to create stellar results.

Tracy Isaak of northern Canada shares her journey on the road to leadership, and how enthusiasm is the secret to building a supportive team. Utah's *Colleen Sorensen* offers tips for escalating issues up the chain of command and thriving in the face of worst-case scenarios. Despite facing discrimination, *Marie-Jo Caesar* from Guadeloupe shares how connecting teams diplomatically helped her create a winning atmosphere. Employee recognition helped *Nanette Bosh,* from Connecticut, build a strong team. Polish-Canadian *Agatha Starczyk* shares an example of poor leadership that motivated her success as an effective leader.

No one succeeds in business alone. Learn from the experiences of these female leaders how effective team leadership can accelerate your success.

Tracy Isaak

Tracy is an energetic Speaker, Certified Success Coach, and Transformational Trainer with over 25 years of combined leadership experience in Health Care Management and Network Marketing.

Known for her contagious radiant energy, humor and sparkling attitude, she possesses the unique ability to empower and inspire others. An unwavering desire to positively impact the lives of many, was the catalyst for Tracy to pursue her entrepreneurial dream. Now the Founder of Isaak Group Training and Development, she assists clients in defining their journey to success and then teaches them how to reach their highest potential.

www.tracyisaak.com

SECTION THREE: CHAPTER ONE

Enthuse Your Team

by Tracy Isaak

> *"A mediocre idea that generates enthusiasm will go further than a great idea that inspires no one."*
> *Mary Kay Ash*

"I'll do it!" I blurted out before my brain bothered to kick in. What was I thinking? Obviously, I wasn't.

I had just volunteered to be the manager of a department that had spiralled into a nasty funk. Staff felt overworked and undervalued. They walked around as if they were serving a prison sentence, as opposed to their careers in health care. Morale had hit rock bottom while blaming and complaining had blown through the roof. Negativity was the full course meal—every day.

I heard horror stories of other young, inexperienced employees who bravely stepped into similar management positions and failed miserably. For whatever reason, I felt compelled to take the risk and move from follower to leader. It felt right in my heart but made absolutely no sense in my head.

I will share with you how I, while using actions and enthusiasm to inspire others, turned our department into the most desired area to work in the organization.

Leadership has a place in your life.

Enthusiasm Beats Knowledge

Who was I to manage a $1 million budget? The family finances I handled were nowhere near $1 million dollars! Who was I to respond to complex labour issues? My only experience with the word 'labour,' was my not-so-pleasant memory of bearing two strapping boys.

Who was I to manage co-workers whose combined experience and education totalled more than the population of my small hometown? The only people managing I had done was family 'management'; meals, housework, laundry and kids activities. How was I going to juggle the extra duties, responsibility and time required to fulfill this role with little or no experience? I felt lost.

I didn't have the answer to these questions, but I did have an immense enthusiasm to work with passion to make a positive difference. If I could enthusiastically win people's hearts and rebuild their belief in themselves and each other, we could change the culture of the department together.

My focus was creating a positive environment for ourselves and those we served. It worked!

Begin by Leading Yourself and Appreciating Others

> *"True leadership mastery begins when you FLY,*
> *First Lead Yourself." Elizabeth McCormick*

Any team will inevitably fail if you do not engage, appreciate and acknowledge their value.

The initial step to leading others is to lead yourself. I worked at becoming a leader others would want to follow by immersing myself in personal development books and courses. As fate would have it, a new senior manager was another blessing. Her core values were to invest in people and develop their skills through leadership training. "Sign me up!" I exclaimed, as I eagerly buried myself in her training tools and knowledge. Soon, coaching and mentoring became a daily win-win.

I managed to squeeze a few bucks out of the budget to reward staff with acts of appreciation for their dedication and commitment. Creatively, those dollars were used for items such as: new supplies and equipment, catered team lunches, casual Fridays, recognition for years of service and a holiday gift for each team member, to name a few. These were simple acts, yet their impact was enormous. Appreciation yielded powerful results—it engaged and united us as a team.

My best chance of success was to 'rally' the troops by acknowledging the value in each team member. Without engagement from the staff, failure would be inevitable. I strived to be more 'interested' than 'interesting' by initiating an open-door-communication policy. I made a daily personal commitment to ask questions, listen actively and get to know people.

These acquired skills have become
invaluable in my career.

Develop Your Core-Transformational Strategies

> *"Become the kind of leader that people would follow voluntarily, even if you had no title or position."*
> *Martin Luther King*

Voluntary follow-ship was critical. I created core transformational strategies that aligned with my personal values. I began with transparency and the almighty dollar...aka the 'budget.' I believed that if I was willing to be forthcoming and share the financials with the team, they would endeavor to stay within the budget and understand its importance and the parameters we had to work within.

I printed out the financial spread sheet for the department, conducted a long overdue staff meeting and asked for input on how and where to allocate the portions of remaining dollars in our budget. It was important for staff to feel comfortable asking for what they needed to complete their jobs, and I assured them this was also a priority for me. To my delight, a positive shift began unfolding right before my eyes. I knew we were on the right track.

In any transformation, accepting responsibility and being flexible to change is crucial. This ultimately instills ownership, promotes growth, and leads to self-empowerment. For those in my department willing to take on additional responsibility and go above and beyond their job description, we collaboratively brainstormed flexible schedules and achievable workloads. Designing flexible work days and daily schedules, while maintaining productivity, created harmony between staff's home and work life.

Happy staff created a positive work environment. Employees were recognized and congratulated at staff meetings and in our newsletter for their efforts. Within six months, sick time and special leaves went down by 30 per cent. Another win-win for all!

Accepting Feedback

Enthusiasm is clearly contagious. To progress as a team, we needed to offer and accept feedback willingly, without feeling offended or judged. That process started with me. I had to set the example if I wanted staff to get involved and be willing to follow my lead.

Feedback for me, not from me, was always the first task on the agenda. I felt that if I were the first to be vulnerable, others would feel more comfortable with the process. One day, a member of my staff pointed out that she loved my enthusiasm, and would appreciate if I could respond to her requests in a more timely fashion. Ouch...she was right. I adjusted accordingly, and demonstrated that I could course-correct using feedback.

Last and most importantly, was customer-service excellence. The main rules for this strategy were simple; stay positive and don't blame or complain. If words were not positive, we were challenged to reframe them. It was essential for everyone to understand that a favourable experience for our clients would benefit everyone. This was the most impactful of all strategies; when staff feels fulfilled in their work, it creates a sense of achievement, engagement and satisfaction. This was quick to implement and it worked excellently.

Customers started to notice a difference, and they jumped on our contagious positive perspective. A stream of compliments and random flower bouquets came in along with the occasional box of chocolates. A LOT of chocolates! All of this came from our happy, satisfied clients who wanted to express their appreciation for our efforts. Many clients had chosen to drive over two hours on icy winter roads to have their diagnostic tests performed by our pleasing first-class staff, as opposed to having the same test performed by a competitor just 10 minutes from their home.

Unexpectedly, one of our senior executives asked me to meet. Scary thoughts of "What did I do wrong?" and "Did I overstep my boundaries?" filled my head. Much to my surprise, what transpired were compliments to the staff and the exceptional service we were providing. He questioned, "What is your department doing down there to make this shift?" Wow, I didn't see that coming! After further discussion, he admitted he was meeting to 'pick my brain' so he could understand how to create a similar transformation in other departments.

Lead by Example and Listen

"When you talk, you are only repeating what you already know. But if you listen, you may learn something new." Dalai Lama

I was amazed at the results that followed implementation of these key-transformational strategies I had learned. Staff felt valued and gratified that they played an active role in making decisions that affected the department's growth. Extrapolating and utilizing the team's knowledge was vital to our success.

Suggestions from team members were eagerly welcomed, which encouraged more ideas, collaborations, and better outcomes. Listening to each new idea became a daily action item contributing to a larger master plan.

By truly believing in each team member, we nourished their belief in themselves. Many positive changes occurred within the group, me included. Trust and comradery were established. Productivity increased and sick time followed a downward curve. A department that once consumed a full course meal of negativity, now enthusiastically dined on caviar of positivity. Our department became the most desired area to work in our organization. Outsiders wanted to be part of our team as we set the new standard.

Create Change with Little Resistance

> *"Success isn't just what you accomplish, it's about what you inspire others to do." Tracy Isaak*

With enthusiasm and a contagious get 'er done attitude, each challenge took on an affirmative spin. There was no 'I' in team, and the success that transpired was due to an amazing group of individuals who willingly followed the lead of enthusiasm and positivity.

Engaged and excited, a zero tolerance for negativity was established. Positivity flowed throughout, and we turned previously so-called catastrophes into valuable lessons. We simply changed our mindset and asked ourselves, "Does this really matter in the big picture?" Thoughts of "What went wrong" turned into "What went right?" It was amazing to participate and observe the evolution of our team and the ripple effect it had in our lives, both in-and-outside the organization.

The strategies we put into action helped team members survive the fast-paced life that we can so easily get caught up in.

Moving Forward Despite Risk

Unbeknownst to me, coaching and mentoring my co-workers using my newly acquired success strategies, would prove to be a pivotal turning point in my career and mindset as a leader and future entrepreneur.

The personal growth and fulfillment I experienced leading with passion and enthusiastically assisting others with their personal transformations will stay with me forever. The experience proved I had uncovered something phenomenal, and it felt so natural.

By overcoming my tolerance for risk, boldly stretching myself, gaining confidence, finding my passion and embracing my newfound courage, I had what I needed to finally start my own business. If you can use your actions and enthusiasm to inspire others to achieve their dreams, then believe me, leadership has a place in your life.

I challenge you to identify your success strategies, breakthrough barriers to risk and explore your leadership possibilities with enthusiasm and positivity.

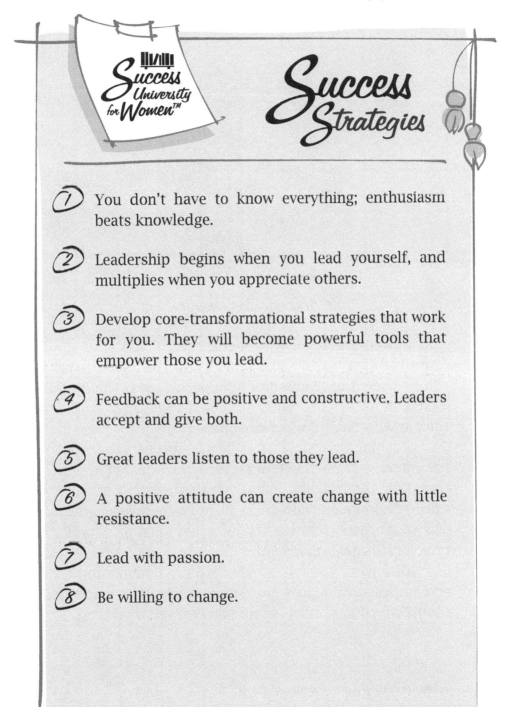

Success Strategies

1. You don't have to know everything; enthusiasm beats knowledge.

2. Leadership begins when you lead yourself, and multiplies when you appreciate others.

3. Develop core-transformational strategies that work for you. They will become powerful tools that empower those you lead.

4. Feedback can be positive and constructive. Leaders accept and give both.

5. Great leaders listen to those they lead.

6. A positive attitude can create change with little resistance.

7. Lead with passion.

8. Be willing to change.

Colleen Sorensen

Colleen believes that "leadership is communicating to people their worth and potential so clearly that they come to see it in themselves." (Stephen Covey) She has a passion for helping others find their voice, their path, their inner strength or personal power.

Teaching soft skills is Colleen's specialty, as she has witnessed firsthand how fast someone can fail when they lack those skills. Through experiential learning, Colleen allows individuals to identify their strengths and weaknesses, creating self-awareness and an action plan for future development.

With over 20 years' experience as an administrator and professor in higher education, Colleen has helped thousands of individuals reach higher levels of success.

www.colleenmoonsorensen.com

SECTION THREE: CHAPTER TWO

Step Up to Responsibility

by Colleen Sorensen

> *"If I have to face something, I do so no matter what the consequences might be."* Rosa Parks

*U*niversity students often complain about their results on classroom exams. But one particular complaint was different; my employee could tell from the student's heartfelt approach that she should re-score the exam just to relieve the student's concerned face. After quickly running the exam through a second machine, a different score registered. To be safe, it was scored on a third machine, producing a third and different score.

How could this happen?

We calibrate our machines on a regular basis and conduct routine maintenance. Since opening, more than 10 million exams were scored correctly at our center. We immediately opened an internal investigation to diagnose the problem.

It was one-third of the way into the semester, and we had already scored and returned over 40,000 exams. As the center's director, several nightmarish scenarios started playing like headlines in front of my eyes. Despite all of the hard work and efforts of a large testing center to ensure we maintain highly efficient systems, there are many enemies who would love to see us fail or close our doors. By the end of the day, my worst fears were realized. Our scoring system was not accurately scoring all exams, and there was no rhyme or reason as to why the errors were happening.

Our entire reputation was built on accuracy and reliability —now in jeopardy. Stress enveloped my body; I couldn't eat, sleep or think clearly. There was no way to know how many students had dropped classes because of inaccurate grades; grades based on tests we were responsible for. A student threatened suicide one day by attempting to jump off a building on campus. My mind raced…what if his incorrectly scored tests led him to this decision? The situation weighed on me night and day. Everything was in question. Nothing was at rest. Pressure to find an answer was overwhelming.

My team began an intensive search for a 'needle in a haystack,' reviewing every possible cause. Multiple specialists were consulted. We retrieved all previously scored tests from every professor and hand-scored each one. To my relief, this painstaking process proved only about 5% of university students were affected, a huge relief. After two weeks, we discovered the problem: a printing press misalignment.

There is a saying, 'Not my circus, not my monkey.' My interpretation of this statement is, "Thank goodness this is not my mess to clean up." Yet what do you do when you realize it is your circus, it is your monkey? All of us are guilty of making mistakes, or simply forgetting something critical to our jobs. On many occasions, including this one, I've experienced that sick feeling in the pit of my stomach the moment I realized that I have missed something vital to my job and need to inform my superiors. If and/or when this happens to you, you can take steps to make the best of the situation.

I want to share a simple game plan I learned to help you navigate these situations, with the intent of coming out the other side holding onto your reputation and retaining trust with your boss.

Establish Expectations Early

In the first few months of establishing a trusting relationship with your supervisor, most are patient while you learn the office climate and culture, and are ready to answer a variety of questions you may ask about how to handle various situations. During this opportunity window, consider asking some of the following questions in your onboarding process:

1. Do you have a document that outlines your expectations of your employees?

2. Is there ever a reason to contact you outside of business hours? If yes, how do you want me to do that?

3. When is it appropriate to interrupt you in a meeting, a phone call, etc.?

4. What things are considered a crisis, what can wait, and how do you want me to distinguish between them?

5. Do you expect me to handle all crises when you are unavailable? Do you want me to notify you of how I handled them?

TIMING: The Sooner, the Better

With the scoresheet problem now identified, my next question was, "How do I break this news to the Vice Presidents?" As my colleagues and I discussed ways to notify the executive team, they all looked at me with sympathy and shared their relief that they were not sitting in my shoes.

One staffer boldly suggested we not say anything at all, "Why bother telling the leadership when we have already fixed the issue?" It was her department and she was afraid of the backlash and possibly losing her job. However, I knew they needed to be informed quickly, before the information spread.

When deciding whether to share an issue with your manager, ask yourself this question,

"If I were in my supervisor's shoes, would I want to know about this?"

If you are unclear, ask additional questions to clarify and establish clear boundaries.

Keep doubt at bay and approach your manager before others do. If you are second, third, or further down the list of informants, you can almost bet your boss will lose trust in you.

Think of it like ripping off a bandage—the faster you do it, the faster you get over it.

When using this tactic, every obstacle may rise up to deter you from having the conversation with your boss or employee. Whether it's bad timing, not knowing what to say, or fear of ramification, beware of conscious or subconscious excuses. Don't delay; take responsibility and share the news.

Each situation is unique, but the sooner you address the issue with your supervisor or employee, the sooner you can get the situation out in the open.

Mental Preparation

> *"Without the strength to endure the crises, one will not see the opportunity within; it is within the process of endurances that opportunity reveals itself."*
> Chin-Ning Chu

Entering your boss's office or a boardroom full of executives can be scary; mental preparation is vital.

When approaching your boss, use visualization or a verbal mantra to focus on positive intention. I imagine my boss and I sitting on the same side of the table, shoulder-to-shoulder. I remove all negative thoughts, and 'what ifs,' take a few deep breaths and imagine an outcome that will please us both.

Listen to your inner voice. Is it positive or negative? When you recognize negative thoughts, replace them with reminders of self-love, and a recognition that you are doing the best you can at this moment. Also, recognize your willingness to rectify the situation, no matter what it takes.

Take 100% Responsibility

> *"Just because you fail once doesn't mean you're gonna fail at everything."* Marilyn Monroe

As the director, the buck ultimately stopped with me. It was up to me to inform the executive team about the testing center crisis. I could have shifted the blame to others, but then I would not own my responsibility as leader. I could have pointed my finger at our printing vendor, our third-party software company who chose to change printing vendors, or others involved in that decision. Yet, in my mind and the minds of the executive team, I was fully responsible for my department.

There is a saying that 'when you point your finger at someone else, there are three fingers pointing back at you.' Taking 100 per cent responsibility means completely owning the issue, and learning from it so we do not repeat the same mistake. It also means fully disclosing one's actions.

As a boss, it's frustrating when an employee omits her part in the situation and I discover those details from others. As leaders, we have an example to set. When we take 100% responsibility in our lives and our work, we show others it can be done.

Another way we take responsibility is by creating possible or completed solutions to the problem before meeting with management. Devising possible solutions ahead of time shows the executive team you are solution-focused and invested in the company's success.

Get Straight to the Point

> *"When a leader is straightforward in saying the toughest stuff, people assume (rightly) that he or she will be courageous in all kinds of essential ways: making difficult decisions; taking responsibility for them; apologizing for mistakes."* Erika Anderson

Never 'beat around the bush' when delivering bad news; there is no need for niceties, compliments, random conversation about the weather or anything else. Supervisors can often read your body language and tell when you are stalling; that awareness may shift the energy in the room to a negative direction. Get straight to the point.

The day I sat across the table from men in dark suits, I had no idea how to break the news gently. As I panned the room, several lines swirled around my head. I took a deep breath, dove right in, and shared the bullet points of the situation. Next, I suggested proposed solutions. Looking across the table, there were wide eyes, deep sighs, mumblings, and rubbing of foreheads. Yet, after sharing our plan, they had little left to say. They thanked me for the update and asked I keep them informed of my progress.

Manage your Emotions

> *"Character cannot be developed in ease and quiet. Only through experience of trial and suffering can the soul be strengthened, ambition inspired, and success achieved." Helen Keller*

I wanted to break down and sob in front of those suits, but I knew that would not accomplish my purpose.

It is critical that you manage your emotions to signal your supervisor that she can trust you and your abilities. Tears, yelling, silence, redundant apologizing, swearing, self-deprecating and other displays of emotion distract from the issue at hand.

A common emotion is defensiveness, or the need to explain why you did what you did or did not do in the situation. While it's a fundamental human need for others to understand us, it's important to recognize when and where it is appropriate to seek this validation.

Not all supervisors are able to manage the employee first, and the issue second. Seek validation elsewhere and focus on the issue. Remember, supervisors are human too; we all have issues, bad days, and moments of weakness.

Receive Feedback Openly

Be open to receive additional suggestions and directives, and take notes on all points of the conversation to ensure you capture any action items they identify. Follow through with every part of the action you propose to maintain trust in the future.

As the executive team requested, I kept them informed as the situation developed and apprised them of any changes.

If your supervisor gives you feedback, quickly share your gratitude and take note of it. The natural tendency is to explain your logic, perhaps becoming defensive. Unless your manager asks for your thoughts on the matter, he may not want your explanation. Simply receive the feedback and thank him for sharing. When I provide feedback to my employees, it is refreshing to hear any of the following responses:

- A simple apology for what happened
- An acknowledgement from the employee for her role in the situation
- A willingness to understand the situation from my perspective
- Confidence to learn from the incident and take different actions in the future.

Follow Up First

Establish a 'next steps' plan regarding the situation, and follow up before your supervisor does.

Make the issue safe to discuss with your boss when you approach her and share what you have done to change or improve the situation. By doing this, you give your supervisor the confidence that you are taking responsibility and learning from the experience.

My Truth

In the case of our scoring system debacle, it was a stressful, trying experience that I do not wish upon anyone. I had no idea if I would leave that boardroom with my job intact. Now, grateful to have survived the crisis, I recognize some important life lessons.

Thankfully, while our center took a hit in usage and trust from our constituents, we recovered in those relationships and overall volume within one semester. I had nightmares of that disaster haunting the center for years, yet surprisingly, the issue has never been used against the center. It was a catalyst for change in some of our business systems, and it showed me the true character of my team.

Everyone makes mistakes, no matter our age or experience. It is painful to admit our errors, regardless of who is to blame. The real test is in the recovery process; what we do once we learn of the errors. People can sense something is wrong when you hide information, so fully disclose the situation. This mistake was costly for both our budget and reputation, but had I not taken responsibility and fully informed our executive team quickly, it could have been much worse. I am human, and I owned that every step of the way. Given I had nothing to hide in the process; my constituents were mostly forgiving and willing to continue doing business with me the following semester.

I attribute my success to sharing my full disclosure, listening to feedback, owning the issue 100 per cent, and fixing it as quickly as I could. These strategies have worked for me and I wish the same for you.

You can step up to responsibility.

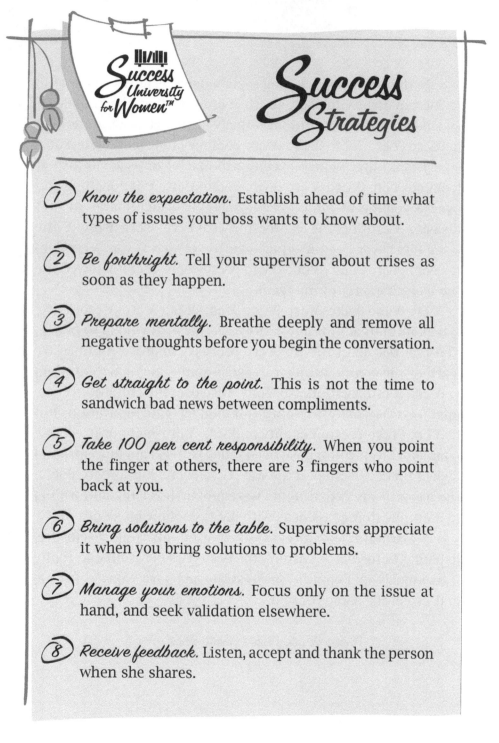

Success University for Women™

Success Strategies

① *Know the expectation.* Establish ahead of time what types of issues your boss wants to know about.

② *Be forthright.* Tell your supervisor about crises as soon as they happen.

③ *Prepare mentally.* Breathe deeply and remove all negative thoughts before you begin the conversation.

④ *Get straight to the point.* This is not the time to sandwich bad news between compliments.

⑤ *Take 100 per cent responsibility.* When you point the finger at others, there are 3 fingers who point back at you.

⑥ *Bring solutions to the table.* Supervisors appreciate it when you bring solutions to problems.

⑦ *Manage your emotions.* Focus only on the issue at hand, and seek validation elsewhere.

⑧ *Receive feedback.* Listen, accept and thank the person when she shares.

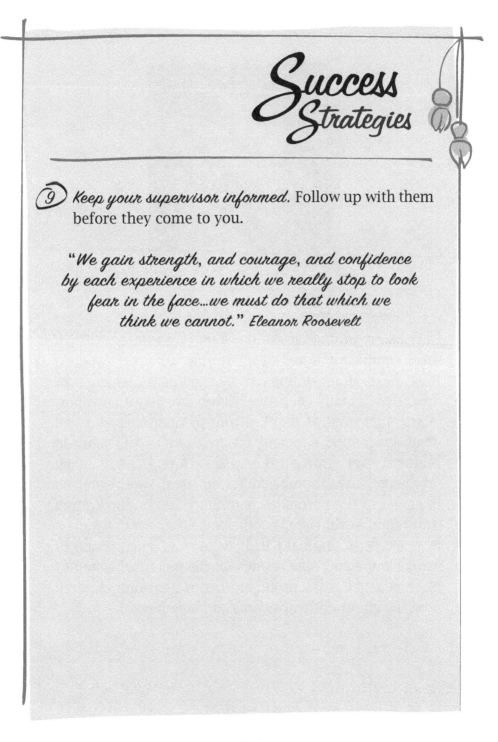

Success Strategies

9) *Keep your supervisor informed.* Follow up with them before they come to you.

"We gain strength, and courage, and confidence by each experience in which we really stop to look fear in the face...we must do that which we think we cannot." Eleanor Roosevelt

Marie-Jo Caesar

Marie-Jo Caesar is the Chief Operating Officer of a significant financial institution. She is a pioneer; instrumental in setting up the company, which now operates in many countries. Passionate about pensions, Marie-Jo served at the forefront of many pension and legislative initiatives and has worked in the pension industry for thirty-three years. Along with being authentic and approachable, she is a well-respected member of the Bermuda community and an inspiration to women world-wide.

Marie-Jo originally hails from the French island of Guadeloupe and now resides on the beautiful island of Bermuda. She is the proud mother of two adult children and the grandmother of three adorable boys.

SECTION THREE: CHAPTER THREE

Connect with Finesse

by Marie-Jo Caesar

> *"Life does not happen...life is a choice."*
> *Marie-Jo Caesar*

*T*here is a lot to be said about being a middle child. As a young adult, I always wondered why my parents relied so much on my opinions. I had a chance to ask them before they passed on; and their answers were similar. My father viewed me as a fair and reliable child who went through unnecessary lengths to garner a consensus on the simplest decisions. My mother thought I was very responsible and gifted with the "patience of Job," remembering I had realistic expectations.

Being a middle child taught me how to compromise and think diplomatically because I had to give up a lot to my big brother and little sister. So, to have my way without upsetting anyone and make my opinion count, I became a strategist and a tactician. I spent a lot of my time getting buy-in from my siblings. I found a way to bring them together in order to reach a consensus which usually resulted in a win-win situation for all concerned. When I could not have my way I handled disappointment well.

Looking at where I am now, I would say that leaders are neither born nor made; leadership is a choice to unify people around us.

Unity Creates Success

As a teenager in secondary school participating in basketball, I decided to prevent what could have been a dreadful situation for my team. A few days before a qualifying game, some of my team mates, lead by the class bully, decided to harm a key player from the other team. They thought they could win the game by tripping her 'accidentally.'

When I heard about the plot, I had to use diplomacy and conciliation to turn a conspiracy into a strategy. I managed to convince my team mates that all the training and sacrifices we made to get that far will only pay off if we entered the court with a winning attitude and ready to apply the tactics and stratagem that we were taught.

Needless to say my idea was frowned upon as tripping a key player seemed to be more effective and guaranteed. I explained that our team mate responsible for this negative action would probably be discovered, thus revealing the collusion and incriminating the entire team. My team mates realized it was in the best interest of the whole team to unite and win the game by focusing our energy on winning the game; and that we did. We had to unite in order to be successful.

> *"United we stand, divided we fall."*
> *Aesop's The Four Oxen and the Lion*

Many years later I married a man who I thought was my partner for life. Unpredictable events occurred and we had to part ways, after two kids and many years of marriage. It was the most uneventful divorce I ever heard of and I made it so for the sake of the kids. I ensured that despite our differences, we remained united since unity is the key to a successful agreement. We attended all schools' events, small and large, important and insignificant as well as major family gatherings. It took a lot of dialogue with my ex-husband to help him see the merit of being unified and the potential concerns the kids might have should their parents not support them by attending their school activities. I had to find common ground by reinforcing the qualities and values that kept us together while working hard to resolve matters that divided us. As a result, our kids are well balanced and do not appear to have suffered much from what could have been a life shattering experience for young adults.

When working with people who have different backgrounds, experiences and personalities, it can be difficult to find common ground. Rule out potential resentment from the beginning by seeking buy-in from all parties.

To be successful, share common goals, involve all players, and focus on solutions that benefit those concerned.

Challenge the Status Quo

My father, a proud family man took his role as head of the family unit seriously. He was an assertive disciplinarian who no one, not even my mother, tried to cross. Little did he know that his small daughter would one day change his decision-making process. Without seeking anyone's opinion, my dad decided nearly all of our family outings. Everyone acquiesced until he wanted to go somewhere the rest of us did not want to go and no one dared say a thing. One day, I brought my mother and siblings together and helped them understand that dad decided for all of us because we let him. All we needed to do was suggest we would rather stay home that day. Although they agreed with me, none of them had the courage to approach my dad, thinking they might upset him. It took courage to challenge the status quo, determination and resilience to take a stand, and a level of commitment to do what was right for the rest of us. I took action with discernment and finesse so that I would not invalidate nor diminish my father's authority and the rest of my family's inability to voice their opinion. From that day onward, dad always consulted with the family before making a decision that concerned all of us.

After completing my tertiary education, I left my home country of Guadeloupe and moved to Bermuda to settle with my Bermudian husband. What an experience! It quickly became clear to me that visiting Bermuda as a tourist and moving to Bermuda as a resident were two different experiences. Thus began my professional life. Before I knew it, I, a French-speaker became a significant 'player' in corporate, English-speaking Bermuda in the eighties and the nineties, when it was a 'white men's world.' I faced many challenges, but also recognition and acknowledgement from an entire white and male board room. I felt the obligation and the responsibility to unify my team and ensure that every staff member was fully engaged in fulfilling the company's purpose while making them feel appreciated for their contribution. My efforts paid off, as the company I manage has skyrocketed from the barest beginnings in 1996 to, today, handling $800 million of client pension funds.

Challenging the status quo can be daunting. To move forward, despite difficulty, always meet challenges head on. Focus on the positive, ignore the negative, build productive habits, believe in your human potential, and adopt an upbeat attitude.

Consistently exude confidence to develop a frame of mind that will enable you to take informed risks.

Responsibilities of Leadership

Unifying leaders encourage those who feel afraid and anxious. They love the unlovable. They strive to understand the arrogant, and egocentric. They protect those who are vulnerable. Unifying leaders are effective facilitators and great communicators. They ask questions. They debate respectfully, logically and in good faith.

As a leader, it's my job to direct my team to the best of my ability, champion my human capital (team) while enhancing my financial capital. To be successful, I have had to unite staff and stakeholders from very different backgrounds and cultures as our organization operates in many jurisdictions. Being a non-English speaker, I have to listen intently to others' ideas, which slows me down, allows me to focus on what is being said, and think about my response.

As leaders we need to be patient, diplomatic, considerate of others when making decisions, and able to comprise.

How do you get nine administrators located in three different jurisdictions to share common goals and meet essential frequent deadlines? Communication, dialogue, and unity are vital tools. Especially when each jurisdiction is led by strong individuals who seem to be concerned about what work for them rather than what works for the operation. Like you, we employ a variety of team members, including some with large egos that express themselves well, are very verbose, and good at rhetoric, while others struggle with self-worth and confidence.

> *To be a successful leader, you must guide others to fulfill their roles, despite challenging personality styles.*

You have to understand people, know how they work, and maximize their strengths. It is rewarding to 'pull' others along in constructive fashion.

Every Player has a Role

Everyone in my 'shop' has a role to play in the success of the company and success does not come without understanding. I pay everyone and they contribute. The challenge: finding the best way to amplify their strengths. Size up your audience, know your players, and give everyone an opportunity.

Also, I empower each employee with accurate guidelines so they understand their role on the team and that every one's job is as important as the other's.

In order for the team to gain traction, I must clearly define all work processes, set my expectations, share the bigger vision and ensure that everyone is fully engaged…even the notoriously uncommunicative ones. How do I engage them? It's a matter of knowing where to place them.

Introverted employees are generally better listeners. However, they often put up their shield because they don't think they have anything to add over the louder voices. When I need several people's feedback or opinion on an issue or potential solution, I engage the more silent ones first. They may offer three words instead of ten sentences and those may be the keywords. If they understand where I want to go, I appoint them as a team leader. There is often a lot of noise, and appointing the silent ones as leaders ensures they will be heard over the more intimidating employees.

In adopting such an approach, they are better equipped to comprehend the importance of the role they play as a team member and the significance of collaboration. This enables the team to consistently meet their monthly deadlines by achieving a smooth and seamless workflow. As John Maxwell said: "Teamwork makes the dream work..."

Don't be afraid to change where someone is placed if it's not working. Team spirit is based on dedication, loyalty and the ability to allow each team member to have a sense of inclusion and kinship.

"Great leaders don't set out to be a leader...they set out to make a difference. It's never about the role—always about the goal." Lisa Haisha

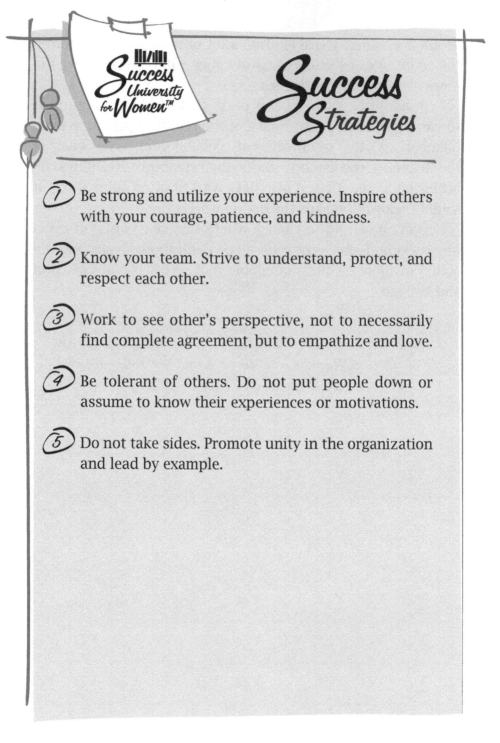

Success University for Women™

Success Strategies

1. Be strong and utilize your experience. Inspire others with your courage, patience, and kindness.

2. Know your team. Strive to understand, protect, and respect each other.

3. Work to see other's perspective, not to necessarily find complete agreement, but to empathize and love.

4. Be tolerant of others. Do not put people down or assume to know their experiences or motivations.

5. Do not take sides. Promote unity in the organization and lead by example.

Notes

Nannette Bosh

Nannette Bosh is an energetic speaker and marketing empowerment expert, teaching entrepreneurs how to grow and maximize their brand presence. She is the Founder of HowtoSchool.net and GoOnlinePro.co. She has been featured countless times in print, radio and televised media including a CBS Prime-Time Special.

Nannette's ability to inspire and connect, along with a motivational style of post writing, earned her a worldwide social media ranking by grader.com among the Top 50 Facebook® Elite, alongside Mashable Founder Pete Cashmore and Premier Facebook® Marketing Expert Mari Smith.

A philanthropic married mother of two, Nannette recently launched the SmallBusinessesCare.org network.

www.nannetteboshinc.com

SECTION THREE: CHAPTER FOUR

Lead Without Ego

by Nannette Bosh

> *"Leadership is being bold enough to have vision and humble enough to recognize achieving it will take the efforts of many people—people who are most fulfilled when they share their gifts and talents, rather than just work." Kathy Heasley*

Feedback is Fuel

In 2001, I read a business magazine article about a company that was finally in a position to offer its' employees a 401k program with dollar for dollar matching. Before they launched the program they polled the employees to find out what they wanted.

As Chief Financial Officer at the time, I knew the importance of a retirement account as part of your overall financial success. To my surprise this company's employees opted for a beverage vending machine with unlimited access to cold drinks in lieu of a 401k plan. I was shocked. Was I assuming things about my staff instead of seeking their feedback?

Leaders are a Work in Progress

One night I couldn't sleep, obsessing over this article. As I tossed and turned I wondered if I was a boss or a leader? I was determined to do something for my employees that a good leader would do.

I'm embarrassed to say we didn't have an employee incentive program at that time. I was determined to put together an acknowledgement program, where both salaried and hourly employees could recognize each other for outstanding performance. I popped out of bed and mapped out my plan.

The next day I arrived early to work and drafted business-sized cards to be printed with an embossed key on them. I've always believed that the employees were the "key" to our company success, so I named the program, "Keys to Our Success." I shared my idea with the team, explaining that anyone caught going above and beyond their job duties and/or lending a helping hand to someone in our organization was eligible for a recognition card. All of the recognition cards were placed in a large bowl for a weekly, monthly and a yearly drawing. The more cards you earned the better your odds of winning. I asked the staff not only for feedback on the program but also for input on the prizes.

> "Real leaders refuse to take the credit for success, but they will always accept responsibility for failures."
> Mike Myatt

Give Them Something to Cheer About

Recognition cards not drawn at the end of the week rolled over from the weekly drawing into the monthly drawing. The monthly prize, valued at $250.00, was displayed near the break area. All cards not drawn at the end of the month then rolled over to the year-end grand prize drawing, a getaway long weekend for two that included spending money and two additional paid days off from work. Every Friday just before close we would all excitedly gather in the shop to draw one card from the bowl for the weekly prize. During each drawing we read and acknowledged what great deed earned the winner his or her card and the shop always filled with applause. The person who issued the acknowledgment card took more delight in the win than the actual winner!

Follow Your Instincts

Everyone in the company was on a mission to find the good in others in order to have the opportunity to issue a card. The staff was upbeat and company morale was at an all-time high. Work was a buzz of efficiency and nobody stood idle.

Whenever there was down time the employees were offering to help each other complete work assignments and get orders out the door. Every Friday you could find the staff cleaning their work areas, even the greasy machines in the shop were clean as a whistle. I was so proud of all of them and the great work they were doing. I was amazed by their loyalty and dedication to the company and to each other.

WOW! Clearly, I now understood what it meant to be a good leader, it was never about me it was about them. I still smile when I think of them today and the lessons I learned about how to lead without ego.

> *"75-80% of our greatest assets walk out the door every single night and we want to make sure they come back." Jim Goodnight*

Know your Assets

Leaders know that great employees are the most valuable assets of any company. It's our job to make sure that the majority of our assets return to work. Our duty as leaders is to understand the wants and needs of our entire team and to remember to express gratitude for employee service and loyalty.

The best way to ensure that happens is to build authentic relationships with those we lead. We must come from a place of service in order to build connections that will last. We cannot simply assume the members of our team want the same things as we ourselves do. We need to be empathetic, take an interest and get to know our staff on a deeper level. We need to listen to what they have to say and look for words left unsaid.

When I was working as a Corporate Leader it was my job to coach the employees and help bring out the best in every associate in order to benefit the entire team. The company motto was "Our family is committed to yours."

One employee was distraught because of personal challenges with her children and their living conditions. When she came to me, we were short staffed, I was buried in work and felt completely overwhelmed. I listened as she shared her dilemma and we put together a solid plan for her family to move forward.

I worked to cover her shifts while she got her house in order. When she returned she was refreshed and relieved. She came to my office with a gift card and a hand-written note stating she had stopped believing in the company motto, but all I had done for her and her family showed her that we stood by our motto. I cried when I read the note and saved it as a reminder that leading often means putting the needs of the team above your own.

Keep Turnover Rate Healthy

According to a study published in the Harvard Business Review, two in five CEO(s) fail in their first 18 months of leading. The Family Firm Institute reports that only 30 percent of family businesses survive the second generation. These are leadership wake up calls!

A small business owner I know had almost "ZERO" employee turnover from the time he founded his company up until the day he retired. This gentleman, compassionate and understanding, came from humble beginnings and knew how to lead without ego. He cherished his employees, treating them with kindness and respect. In return, they gave their heart and soul to the company, the owner and his mission. The employees thought the world of this man and always spoke highly of him. Whenever they were faced with a personal problem he was quick to offer a helping hand. The employees would often say, "He (the owner) would cut off his right arm and give it to any one of us that needed it."

Eventually the owner's son took over the business. Unfortunately, he has an ego so big that he prides himself on demonizing and demoting the employees. This is what the employees say about the founder's son, "He's nothing like his father, he would cut off our arm just so he could have a spare." Many employees have since left the company. Turnover is not only costly; it is a direct reflection on a leader's ability to maintain morale.

> *"Leadership is the ability to not only understand and utilize your innate talents, but to also effectively leverage the natural strengths of your team to accomplish the mission." Katie Christy*

Self-Development is the Turning Point

Some leaders are like the founder and find it easier than others to check their ego at the door. Whether it comes naturally or not, leading without ego is vital to the health of your team and your company.

One way to let go of ego is by working on self-development. As you learn and grow, you will be better equipped to inspire and nurture the talents of your followers.

One way is by committing to continual learning. Take advantage of available self-development courses and books. As you develop yourself, you will become a better leader. In addition to learning, devoting time as a volunteer can help you improve your leadership abilities. Genuinely serving others is rewarding and helps you stay centered in gratitude.

Another way to become a better leader from within is to develop confidence and be transparent. When you are confident, you are unafraid of being wrong or replaced. Confidence in yourself shows others they can have confidence in you. Transparency in leadership reduces follower resistance. When you are transparent and genuine with your team, they know they can trust you as a leader.

> *"Leadership is the ability of one life to positively influence another." Nannette Bosh*

Leadership is the opportunity to make a difference in the lives of many and leave a legacy, provided you're willing to check your ego at the door. Successful leaders express gratitude and are authentic, kind and respectful. They seek ways to improve, learn and grow and empower others to realize their full potential. Great leaders are also humble and empathetic, possessing the ability to understand what it is like to be in the shoes of another.

As a leader the best way to ensure your success and the success of your team is to be willing to lead without allowing your ego to get in your way. It's never about you, it's always about them. Each morning when you greet your team, think about the type of leader you want to be and how you'd like to be remembered. Then ask yourself, will you lead like the founder or his son?

The choice is yours.

Success University for Women™

Success Strategies

1. **Feedback is Leadership Fuel.** We must ask for feedback and be willing to receive it both positive and negative.

2. **Give Them Something to Cheer About.** Your energy is contagious so keep it positive and find ways to help the team celebrate everyone.

3. **Real Growth Takes Time.** The journey toward growth is never ending because we grow as we go.

4. **Always Follow Your Instincts.** You were given a gut instinct for a reason so if it feels right or wrong it is.

5. **Know Your Real Assets.** Those you lead are your real assets and everything else can be replaced.

6. **Keep Your Turnover Rate Healthy.** Successful leaders make morale a priority because they understand the true costs associated with employee turnover.

7. **Self-Development is the Leadership Turning Point.** It is through our own self-discovery that we learn the art of helping others become their best selves.

Notes

Agatha Starczyk

Agatha is a human resources strategist, executive leadership coach, writer and speaker. An experienced business consultant, she has extensive internal and external consulting experience in human resources, talent development and process optimization for various industries. Through her coaching work, Agatha partners with individuals and organizations to improve effectiveness, accelerate results and achieve higher levels of performance. In doing so, she helps individuals become more effective leaders, move ahead in their careers and gain personal satisfaction.

Agatha is an avid volunteer. She is currently serving as the District Commissionaire for the Polish Girl Scouts in Alberta, is involved in other areas of the Polish community as well as the arts in Calgary. She also enjoys travel, baking and exploring the outdoors.

www.praeceptumconsulting.com

SECTION THREE: CHAPTER FIVE

Model Teamwork

by Agatha Starczyk

"Leadership is about making others better as a result of your presence and making sure that impact lasts in your absence." Sheryl Sandberg

*I*n a split second, she lost my respect. I went from excited to angry, disappointed and disheartened. She was supposed to be my leader—she was older, more experienced and someone we were supposed to emulate and admire.

I was twelve years old when my camp leader stood in the middle of the forest demanding we put up her tent, the kitchen and later our own tents. We were attending an annual Polish Girl Scout camp adventure that was supposed to be fun.

Her nagging and yelling were amplified by weeks of pouring rain, hail and cold weather. Scouts and leaders alike were unhappy.

We spent the next two weeks opposing everything she told us to do. I recall us avoiding meals, never cleaning our tents, sneaking out at night and sleeping through our morning alarms. If she wasn't making an effort, why should we? If she was punishing us regardless of how well we performed tasks, why bother doing them at all?

Earn your following

> *"Leadership is not a license to do less; it is a responsibility to do more."* Simon Sinek

After that camp experience and long before I started to work, I promised myself I would expect from others only what I was willing to do.

I swore that when I became a leader, I would pick up tent poles and help the group to put up their tents first, and then my own.

Fast-forward 25 years, I now supervise nearly 20 volunteer leaders who are responsible for over 100 youth in Alberta, Canada. Based on my rank and years of experience, I could sit back and direct their activities while sipping my coffee. I could point out their flaws or simply hide behind my title and yell orders to anyone below me. Instead, I choose to engage my direct reports through conversation and collaboration, and teach leadership by example.

As part of this pattern, our leaders eat meals last, stay awake until the last camper is asleep, and ensure that everything is ready for the next day.

Authority comes with rank and position, but respect for that authority only results from a positive outward example.

Be present

In Polish scouting, we run all of our activities in Polish, and we expect everyone to speak the language to one another when together. Our group is composed of first, second and third generation immigrants. Living outside our native Poland, the language does not necessarily come naturally and many of us revert to English when we are not paying attention. Leaders must set the example. If we are speaking English amongst ourselves, we cannot possibly push the kids to make an effort to speak Polish.

Similarly, in business, a leader must be conscious of the effect her actions have on others. Someone is always watching or listening, and a leader's ability to deal with conflict or a difficult situation will be noticed. These situations require more composure and presence than when things are going smoothly.

If the leader handles the situation well, she can inspire others to do the same.

Find a role model

"Leadership is a series of behaviors rather than a role for heroes." Margaret Wheatley

The individuals I know who lead by example are not perfect, do not always have it together, do not have all the answers and are not always warm and fuzzy. Rather, they are willing to recognize their faults and weaknesses, and are open to asking for and receiving assistance. They are confident in their beliefs and stand their ground, even if their decisions are not popular.

Julia is someone I have known for a long time. A few years ago, she took a position within our organization that was relatively new to her. Although she had some initial reservations, I could not have imagined a better person for the job.

She is someone I always admired for her faith and humility, and since stepping up, I have come to appreciate her even more. She is open about the things she does not know and confident enough to ask for help. She recognizes the important role each team member plays and treats them with respect. This ensures that they have the opportunities to learn and the resources they need to succeed.

Her family is her priority, and thus, she understands the importance of family in the lives of other volunteers. She is deliberate in her communication, and considers the effect of her actions on everyone around her. The group of leaders who report to her, as well as the youth she oversees look up to Julia. Their parents also treat her with the utmost respect. In situations when she has to deliver a difficult message, she is able to remain composed and provide sound reason. The parents have little knowledge of our ranks and titles, yet she has earned their trust through her actions. She is not afraid to try something new alongside everyone else, and above all, she lives the values that scouting is based on, namely service to others.

Be kind to yourself and others

> *"When a leader becomes a martyr for their cause, they stop being a good example."* Agatha Starczyk

Once given the important responsibility of leadership, it does not have to monopolize your life. Just because others' eyes are on you, does not mean you cannot fail. At times, I have overcommitted myself and not been able to follow through, tried to split my time between too many projects and been unable to fulfill them to my standards. When a leader becomes a martyr for their cause, they stop being a good example. They either bring others down with them or turn them away.

Some leaders make sure their teams know about the time they put in and how tired they are as a result. Other leaders, set a better example for their team members by making their boundaries clear, allowing for down time, and setting realistic expectations.

Leadership by example, from our behaviour to the way we communicate and live, is as vital in business as it is in life. The title of leader does not necessarily mean others want to follow you. In any relationship, leading means keeping your word, showing compassion toward others, being respectful, and standing up for your values. Respecting yourself and showing respect for others' time and personal lives is also a key component of being a leader. It means being consistently open and honest and having integrity. Leading successfully results in mutual respect.

Be honest

There are times when we work for people who don't shine as examples of who we'd like to be. Therefore, it is up to us to make the best of the situation. You can rise above when you are conscientious of your tasks, know the expectations of your supervisor, and understand their leadership approach. It may surprise you what you can teach that person.

Situations of stress and conflict can cause even the most composed leaders to behave differently than they would otherwise. When they do, they set the tone and direction of the situation. I have come a long way from when I was easily offended and too quick to react, causing others to do the same. An experienced leader who seeks to set a positive example for her team steps back to evaluate the situation before she reacts. In recent years, I have made a conscious effort to take criticism with a grain of salt, gather all the facts, and approach conflict in a more pragmatic and calm manner. Sometimes this means I wait a night before I send a strong email or seek advice before I jump to conclusions.

Set the example you would follow

At some point in the not so distant future, I plan to move on from my current volunteer positions. I am very proud of my and my team's accomplishments; in a short time, we have grown our organization exponentially without conflict. However, the truest test of my leadership will be what happens next.

Will my example keep my team on this path? Will the leaders who follow be conscious of what they say and how they behave? Will they seek to pass this skill set to future leaders? It is not simply about doing things the same way, but also living the qualities and values so they inspire those around them.

Scouting is a big part of my life and has shaped me into the leader I am. It taught me that leadership comes in many different forms, and the most impactful leaders do not need a title.

They earn respect by being humble and creating an effective model for teamwork.

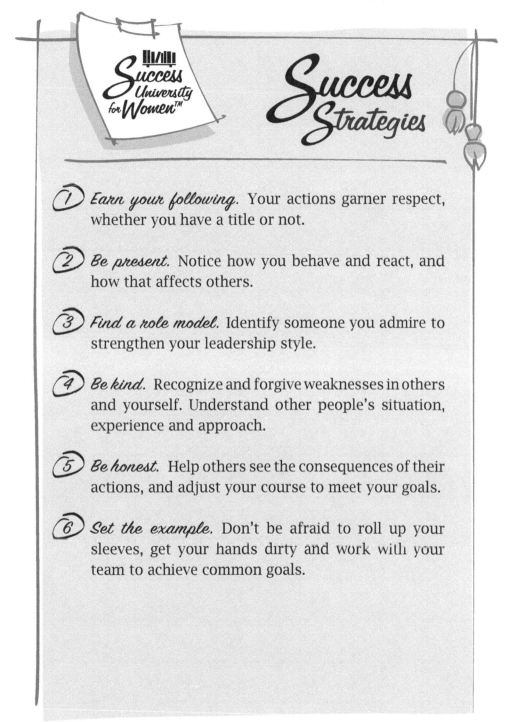

Success Strategies

1. *Earn your following.* Your actions garner respect, whether you have a title or not.

2. *Be present.* Notice how you behave and react, and how that affects others.

3. *Find a role model.* Identify someone you admire to strengthen your leadership style.

4. *Be kind.* Recognize and forgive weaknesses in others and yourself. Understand other people's situation, experience and approach.

5. *Be honest.* Help others see the consequences of their actions, and adjust your course to meet your goals.

6. *Set the example.* Don't be afraid to roll up your sleeves, get your hands dirty and work with your team to achieve common goals.

Section Four

Influencing

SECTION FOUR: INTRODUCTION

*N*ame the woman who influenced you most in your career. She comes to mind immediately, even though she may not be aware of her impact in your life. The experienced leaders in this section share their strategies for positively influencing others.

Kristi Staab of Las Vegas identifies the qualities that draw us to rock stars and the difference between authority and influence. *Gale Weithers* of Barbados shares her strategies for leading the next generation. With decades of experience in hotel management, *Derra Edwards* shares her 'secret sauce' for influencing those up and down the business hierarchy. Retired military officer *Deanna Won* teaches you how to overcome adversity as a woman in business, step into leadership roles and speak your truth. *Success University for Women*™ Co-Founder Jan Fraser shares how intentionally leading others powerfully shapes our legacy.

Learn from these authors how to maximize your influence on future generations, and leave a positive legacy long after you are gone.

We all leave a legacy when we depart this world.
Will your legacy inspire others?

Kristi Staab

Driven by her passion to help people from around the globe transform into to strong, purposeful, impactful, positive, and influential leaders, Kristi shares her innovative and inspiring Lead Like a Rock Star™ approach to discover, hone, and put into action the rock star leader within. It's what Kristi refers to as "Put the rock in your role™."

For more than 25 years, Kristi has been developing individuals, teams, and organizations to excellence in the areas of leadership, sales, and success with a straightforward leadership philosophy.

"Being a rock star is an attitude. It's a state of being. It's a choice. It's raising your hand and committing to being an elite performer, playing at the highest level, reaching the pinnacle of your chosen profession, and modeling excellence consistently to inspire and empower others to do the same."

www.KristiStaab.com

SECTION FOUR: CHAPTER ONE

Exemplify Excellence

by Kristi Staab

> *"Model excellence consistently to inspire and empower others to do the same."*
> *Kristi Staab, leadership expert and executive coach*

P atsy Cline. Aretha Franklin. Carol King. Joni Mitchell. Dolly Parton. These are among the most common female musical legends whose names have been recited for generations when up and coming musicians were asked the question, "Who are your influences?"

Whether influencing musicians in their respective genres and beyond, or transcending the world of music all together, these talented and distinguished women have left their indelible marks on countless artists.

All rock stars leaders in their own right; these influencers have fueled, and will continue to fuel, the ambitions of countless artists over time.

Through their own personal and professional journeys of tragedy and triumph, their actions have served as a source of encouragement, inspiration, and empowerment for others. Blaze new trails. Take risks emotionally and musically. Create and innovate. Become strong, independent businesswomen. Invest it forward.

> *"I want so much for it to go beyond the music for my fans. Inspiration as ambition. How the spiritual laws can affect their lives. And in my own personal life, Deepak [Chopra] has been an amazing friend. He has always reminded me to work in a life of service to my fans and to fulfill my vision and my destiny."*
> *Lady Gaga, American Singer, Songwriter, and Actress*

An Influencer and Legend in the Making

Although Lady Gaga is relatively new to the music scene compared to the legends, she has quickly risen as a rock star musician and leader whose influence extends well beyond the billboard charts.

In 2016, Lady Gaga and former Vice President Joseph Biden traveled around the United States on the "It's On Us" tour, visiting college campuses to highlight the importance of preventing sexual assault. I was fortunate to participate in their stop at the University of Nevada, Las Vegas.

Just a week prior, I had seen an interview with Lady Gaga where she shared that she didn't like taking selfies with fans because to her selfies seemed impersonal; instead, she preferred making more direct, personal connections with people.

As someone who both appreciates her showmanship and is an observer of her influence, leadership, and success, I was appreciative to be able to connect with Lady Gaga one-on-one. Following her performance, she exited the stage and came down into the audience to interact with students and other attendees. Respecting her position on taking selfies, I simply smiled and nodded at her as she approached me. She stopped and stood face-to-face with me, took my hands in hers, looked directly in my eyes and said, "You are a very beautiful woman." She paused and held her eye contact with me as tightly as she did my hands. In addition to the influence she had with the students there on her tour stop that day, she had a profound, personal impact on me that I will never forget. There are no words to express those few moments. Time stood still.

Nearly a year later, I saw her connect in a similar way with a fan on the world's largest stage. While performing to a worldwide viewing audience in the neighborhood of 111 million viewers during the Super Bowl LI halftime show, Lady Gaga left stage and walked among the audience members and put her arm around a young fan. Again, time stood still for the person Gaga connected with one-on-one in that moment.

While standing on the shoulders of giants[1] who have come before her, Lady Gaga's musical and artistic influences have included Queen, Elton John and Andy Warhol. Additionally, she identified Deepak Chopra as her biggest influence in 2010 and credited performer Tony Bennett with saving her life in 2014.

Clearly, Lady Gaga is influenced by other leaders. She had a profound influence on me through our personal connection, and she has influenced others well beyond the music industry.

Who has influenced your leadership over the years? How have they impacted your leadership? How far did their leadership influence extend?

---

[1] *Paraphrased from a quote attributed to Sir Isaac Newton in 1675.*

Rock Star Leaders in Business

While there are plenty of leaders throughout the world, what the world needs now is strong, purposeful, impactful and positively influential leadership in our homes, communities, governments and businesses. I refer to this type of leader as a "rock star" leader. After all, rock stars are standouts. Game changers. Motivators. Leaders. Also defined as the best of the best—in any category.

Let's take a look at the need for rock star leaders in American business today. In the 2017 "State of the American Workplace," the Gallup Organization released data that showed two-thirds of the American workforce is disengaged and their needs are not being met within the organization. Fifty-one percent identified themselves as "not engaged," meaning they lack energy and passion in their work. Sixteen percent identified themselves as "actively disengaged," indicating they are resentful, unhappy and may even undermine the accomplishments of their engaged colleagues. A disengaged employee is estimated to cost her employer $3,000 for every $10,000 in salary.

Not surprisingly, the data illustrated that only one-third of the workforce in America are engaged in their jobs. In other words, only one-third surveyed are passionate about and feel connected to their organization. Engaged employees also experienced higher productivity and customer satisfaction as well as lower absenteeism and turnover than disengaged employees. When the leaders of the organizations themselves are engaged in the workplace, the managers reporting to them are 39 percent more likely to be engaged, while the employees who work for their engaged managers are 59% more likely to be engaged.

What percentage of your workforce is engaged, not engaged, or actively disengaged? How do your organization's results compare with the national average? What are your disengaged employees costing your business today—in absenteeism, turnover, employee morale, and profitability?

> *"Leadership is about making others better as a result of your presence and making sure that impact lasts in your absence."*
>
> *Sheryl Sandberg, Chief Operating Officer at Facebook®*

The Role of Influence in Leadership

Clearly leadership is important to a company's success and long-term sustainability. To better understand leadership, we need to understand influence.

According to internationally recognized leadership expert Ken Blanchard, "The key to successful leadership today is influence, not authority." At the core of influence in leadership, is one's ability to inspire the way others think, believe or behave.

Think about leaders in the workplace, and consider the levels of influence they have on team members at work. At the most basic level, leaders influence how people do their work. For example, leaders ensure team members understand how to perform in their positions and monitor progress on their responsibilities and larger organizational goals.

An even more effective leader may influence how team members within an organization live their lives with regard to their values, health, clothing, relationships, education and more.

A positively influential leader may inspire team members to adjust their personal attributes if the team members are shaped by and choose to include something they like, respect, or admire about the leader into their own experience. This is what I refer to in my work as "taking people beyond their own blinders—their current knowledge, experience, opportunities or possibilities at a particular snapshot in time." This is a chance to share something with your team members that they may not have come across, or may not have even known existed, up to that point in their lives, guiding your team members to learn, grow and develop as well.

At the highest level, truly transformational leaders have an effect on people well beyond their own workplace environment. Due in large part to her professional background and credibility and New York Times Bestseller *"Lean In: Women, Work, and the Will to Lead,"* Sheryl Sandberg's influence transcends past her role within Facebook®, Inc. and even the technological industry, making multiple appearances in the rankings of both Forbes World's 100 Most Powerful Women and TIME 100: The 100 Most Influential People in the World List. She influences people's lives well beyond the workplace and reminds us that our leadership is present even in our absence.

Regardless of who we are or where we have come from, who we are today is a result of those who have influenced us over the course of our careers and lifetimes.

What influence are you having on people as a leader? How will you positively influence the leadership, growth and development of others? How far will your leadership influence extend?

Influence and Rock Star Leaders

Based on my 20-year career in corporate America that spanned the worlds of music, sports, entertainment and business, my Lead Like a Rock Star™ approach to leadership, sales and success focuses on The Nine Essential Elements that Rock Stars Leaders Exemplify™. These are the principles that drive an inspiring leader and leadership philosophy, an effective organizational culture, and a purposeful attitude, state of being, and choice. It's what I refer to as, "Put the Rock in

Your Role™." Simply put, it's modeling excellence consistently to inspire and empower others to do the same—or, in other words, positive influence.

Previous generations of musicians have influenced today's generation and today's generation will influence future generations. After reading this chapter, I hope that as one of today's female leaders, you will commit to positively influencing the current and future generations of female leaders as well. Together, we'll invest it forward.

As leaders, we have the opportunity to make a significant impact through our influence by simply modeling excellence consistently in our homes, communities, governments and businesses. When we do, our influence will continue to inspire and empower others to do the same.

One leader. One influence. One success at a time.

Success University for Women™

Success Strategies

1. Share your journeys of tragedy and triumph to help encourage, inspire and empower others to blaze new trails, take risks, exercise creativity, excel in business and invest it forward.

2. Make personal and meaningful connections with others.

3. Acknowledge and appreciate those who have positively influenced your leadership growth and development over the years.

4. Make every effort to ensure each of your employees are engaged, impassioned, and feel a connection to the organization.

5. Recognize that influence is the key to successful leadership. (Not authority.)

6. Commit to exercising strong, purposeful, impactful and positively influential leadership.

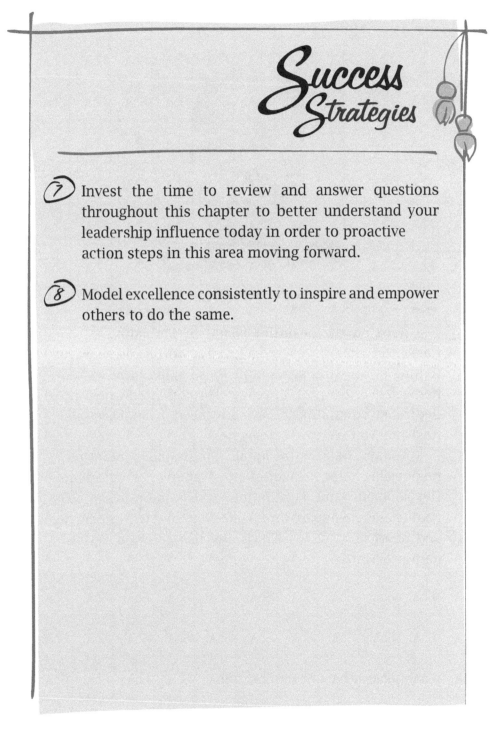

Success Strategies

7. Invest the time to review and answer questions throughout this chapter to better understand your leadership influence today in order to proactive action steps in this area moving forward.

8. Model excellence consistently to inspire and empower others to do the same.

Gale Weithers

Born on the beautiful island of Barbados, in the Caribbean, Gale discovered a love for words and creative writing at an early age. Both these skills have served her well over the past 30 years. Through hard work and dedicated commitment, she advanced from Executive Assistant to Executive Manager.

Today, Gale is a Retail Programmes Manager, responsible for Customer Training Programme Development and Facilitation across more than 20 countries. In her spare time, Gale blogs and writes poetry and short stories, for which she has received several national awards.

www.galeweithers.wordpress.com

SECTION FOUR: CHAPTER TWO

Engage Millennials Successfully

by Gale Weithers

> *"You may not control all the events that happen to you, but you can decide not to be reduced by them."*
> Maya Angelou

After several months of hard work, the day of our regional conference finally arrived. There I stood on stage speaking in front of my entire team which included several millennials. Mid-way through the Customer Service Survey data being shared, I felt an intensely hot pain spread across my chest and knew I was in trouble. Looking out over the 70+ faces in the audience that morning, I tightened my grip on the podium, willing my heartbeat to slow down. Everyone was waiting for me to speak but this was a rare life moment when I struggled to find the right words.

What could I say to this high-level group of managers to help them better understand my message, after my executive publicly expressed his disappointment and concern with my overly 'negative' presentation? Nothing in my more than 25 years' experience as a Presenter and Training Facilitator had prepared me for this. I could not move; I could not speak. The junior members of my team were waiting and watching in shock so I needed to choose my path carefully. I reached for my glass of water.

This experience tested my leadership on two levels: first, wondering how to respond professionally to my executive's remarks and second, how to protect my millennials while encouraging their learning and growth.

We All Start Somewhere

Growing up, I never wanted to be a leader. Why lead when you could simply fall in line safely behind those making the decisions? Following definitely had its benefits. I started my first job almost immediately out of school at 17 years old, willing to be led as I learned everything related to the company's solar energy business. Going out of my way to assist others, I became exposed to valuable information on budgeting, wage calculations, the power of words in memos and emails as well as how to coordinate management meetings.

Over the years, my career eventually brought me face to face with powerful men and women, successfully leading their companies and departments into the future. They never backed down from challenges, were strict but fair in their expectations of their teams, and excellent mentors as well as leadership examples, which in turn, shaped my ability to lead successfully. As a result of these experiences, I encourage everyone to capitalize on each opportunity to learn from others. It does not matter what job you are in or how old you are, there are invaluable life lessons to be learned.

Success Tools for Millennials

One cannot be a follower forever. At some point you will be singled out, as I was, to be a potential leader. Unfortunately, many of today's younger people have not been taught the skills necessary to be successful in their careers or to emerge as leaders. They have to learn as they go.

If you are a young person, the following guidelines will help you become successful when interacting with employers and more mature leaders in your career.

Be willing to accept additional responsibility.

Many young people shy away from accepting more responsibility either because they are afraid of making mistakes, or they don't see a reason to take on more work. If your superiors are willing to trust you with greater responsibility, there are many benefits to accepting it.

A millennial assistant and I were once tasked to produce a comprehensive research document, which involved pulling together information from several different sources. Although labor intensive and outside of our usual scope, the results from the research would guide our department towards better long-term training decisions.

As I began the initial discussions, the resistance and trepidation were tangible. However, we moved forward and over the next few weeks I promoted open conversation while offering guidance and support.

I also emphasized the fact that responsibility for completion within the deadline was not mine. I trusted my assistant to submit the document on time...and he did. It was a learning process for both of us. I learned to delegate and coach more, while he took on more responsibility. In the end, it was a win-win result for both of us.

Pay attention to detail.

As you learn to effectively lead yourself, remember that details matter. Millennials, as a group, often fail to see the importance of details, so this focus will set you apart. Paying attention to detail can mean the difference between a company remaining solvent versus filing for bankruptcy or a conference attendee not having a hotel room available upon arrival.

Slow down and take the necessary time to closely review and analyze figures correctly. As my team learned, the smallest computation error, where sales figures are used as a basis for reward and recognition, can result in the misallocation of significant cash awards.

Learn to be organized.

Keeping your mind and work environment tidy at all times is an important and vital skill. Organization is another trait scoffed at by some young people, but is essential in business. WHY? Managers expect you to be able to locate documents at a moment's notice, and without accurate records customers may be lost. Use efficient systems for organizing paper and digital files so that data and project information will be quickly accessible. When using a digital filing system, ensure you are backing up information regularly and have paper documents available in the event of a dead battery or loss of Wifi access.

Your managers and clients will be impressed when you are organized and prepared at meetings. Being organized is a simple idea that makes a big impact. Do not hesitate to ask your trainer or manager if you need organizational training.

Communicate clearly.

Use specific and supporting details as much as possible in your communication.

Many say that with the millennial generation's growing dependence on technology, face to face communication is suffering. Older managers and supervisors often prefer verbal communication to digital. When you are talking to your supervisor, look her in the eye and share your prepared and organized information as clearly as possible. Also, be prepared to answer additional questions to the best of your ability. If you don't know the answers, let her know you will do research and get back with her by a certain time.

Focus on following up so that everyone is kept 'in the loop' on projects. Do not assume the members of your team or other co-workers know what is going on; make sure you tell them as it is important to keep everyone updated. Top executives can, but do not necessarily have time to track details at a micro level. Recognize the importance of providing regular comprehensive updates and keeping managers abreast of project statuses, even though the information being compiled is already available.

Life Learnings for the More Mature

> *"You should never view your challenges as a disadvantage. Instead, it's important for you to understand that your experience facing and overcoming adversity is actually one of your biggest advantages." Michelle Obama*

We face many challenges in leadership. Age diversity can be a major trial if not managed properly. As a mature manager today I have had to accept that I am different in many ways from the younger millennials who come to my company. Working with these employees can be difficult, but we can overcome the challenges to help them become leaders in their own right.

In spite of our diverse habits, attitudes, perspectives and problem resolution strategies, it is not only our job to learn from each other but more importantly to work together so all can be successful.

As a whole, millennials possess a different mindset surrounding company loyalty and commitment, preferring to have the freedom to chart their own path at will. They would rather not resolve problems requiring in-depth analysis and/or intense concentration. Instead, they prefer the satisfaction of completing several tasks rather than one big one. Finally, it is useful to bear in mind that millennials do not use traditional means of communication readily, leaning towards mobile apps and the latest technology to relay information quickly. Be patient and willing to learn more about the things that interest them without sacrificing company policy or efficiency. We can also help them hone the skill of being able to think on their feet, especially under pressure.

I was pleasantly surprised when a junior member of my team successfully executed a project I assigned.

Hesitant at first, knowing she would be held accountable for the final outcome, her fears were allayed as I communicated relevant details and assured her of full support. During the post event debrief, she expressed her appreciation for the faith I had demonstrated in her ability to get the job done, even while she did not possess this confidence. I was impressed by her honesty and willingness to learn in spite of being stretched beyond her comfort zone. Be open to the lessons and benefits you will find when working with millennials. As you willingly share your knowledge and expertise, you will be taught as well.

Test Yourself Here

Being a leader at any age is challenging, but that does not mean you cannot achieve success. Whether you are younger or more mature here are a few questions to ensure you are on the right path:

1. Do I get desired results? Do I provide clear direction? Am I failing to delegate?

2. Do I create genuine staff relationships by generating and sustaining trust?

3. Do I support, mentor/coach and motivate others?

4. Am I acting unreliably or treating team members inappropriately?

5. What are the life learnings and how can I execute differently going forward?

The Destination is in the Journey

"Turn your wounds into wisdom." Oprah Winfrey

On that unforgettable day while on stage at our regional conference, I elected to make the situation a life-learning event. The most important lesson? Unforeseen circumstances are just that: unforeseen. It is our reaction to these situations which is paramount. After taking a moment to recover my composure, I thanked my executive politely for his feedback, and requested his permission to complete my presentation. His questions—if there were any additional ones—would be answered at that time.

No matter your age or circumstances, the destination is in the journey.

I encourage you to see yourself as a trailblazer, a frontrunner, a creator, an innovator, a coach, a mentor, a champion...a leader.

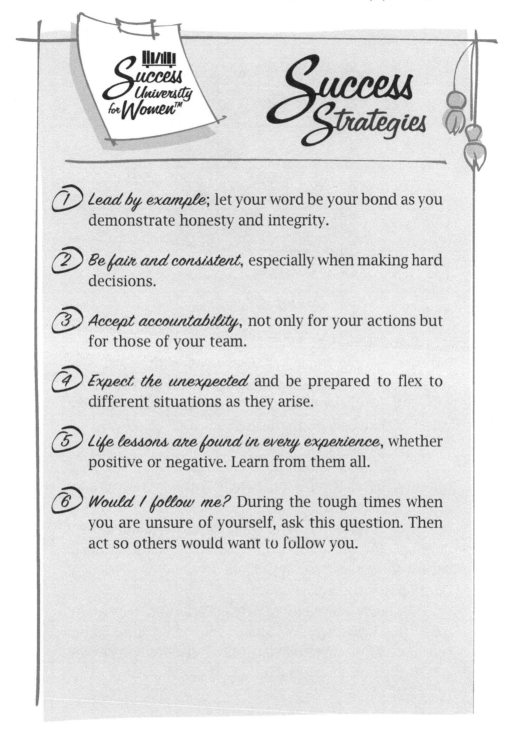

1. *Lead by example*; let your word be your bond as you demonstrate honesty and integrity.

2. *Be fair and consistent*, especially when making hard decisions.

3. *Accept accountability*, not only for your actions but for those of your team.

4. *Expect the unexpected* and be prepared to flex to different situations as they arise.

5. *Life lessons are found in every experience*, whether positive or negative. Learn from them all.

6. *Would I follow me?* During the tough times when you are unsure of yourself, ask this question. Then act so others would want to follow you.

Derra Edwards

Derra Edwards is a veteran in the Hospitality industry leading organizations for over 30 years. She creates and executes learning development programs and initiatives. Her focus is on structuring values-driven cultures that engage the leadership and employees to drive exceptional performance.

Derra is certified in numerous Franklin Covey trainings as well as a Canfield Certified Trainer and program assistant.

Ms. Edwards has held training and organizational development positions with Montage International, Bacara Resort & Spa, Wyndham International/Golden Door Spas and Carefree Resorts.

She holds a Bachelor of Arts in Parks and Recreation from the University of Idaho and after graduation continued at Washington State University, studying Hotel and Restaurant management.

SECTION FOUR: CHAPTER THREE

Seize the Three C's

by Derra Edwards

"Blessed are the Curious for they shall have Adventures." Lovelle Brachman

W hen I was hired in 2002 as the Director of Training for a new luxury hotel brand, we had three short months to the grand opening. The owner had a vision of what he wanted to create with his new company and I was tasked with fulfilling that vision, specifically in the area of employee training. Most of the management team had worked in the hotel industry before and we knew what we liked. Our ultimate goal: provide a memorable guest experience while exceeding expectations.

Culturally, the first task was creating the vision statement and determining the best way to describe our mission. Everything was built upon how the environment and service were going to make the guest feel. Identifying and working on the Values, Vision, Mission, and Service Standards were a huge part of my day. The challenge was how these could be defined and what type of training would instill them in our employees for greater 'buy-in.' We felt sure that if we took care of our employees and guests, and contributed to the community, there was a great chance we would be successful.

After working all day, during this development period, the management team met for 3-4 hours each evening to update the progress in each area of the hotel. There was a great deal of discussion around the best way to hire, develop, recognize, and appreciate employees. Most companies normally award an employee of the month, or employee of the quarter with a special celebration or gift.

Years earlier, I was part of an employee of the month event at a different property and sat next to, Tim, one of the nominees. We had a delightful lunch and wonderful conversation around the table about the nominees and their contributions. When the announcer stood up, introduced the nominees and said, "And the winner for the month is Betty," (not Tim) I physically felt his sadness and disappointment. It was incredibly overwhelming and I thought, "No one should ever feel that way. It's just not right." I could not get the memory out of my head. I knew I had to suggest other possibilities to this new leadership team.

At our meeting one evening, I spoke up, "Whatever the event is, whoever is nominated, whoever is at the dinner, there cannot be a winner that night. There should not be a winner singled out from the group."

Everyone sitting around the table was a little shocked. "What do you mean there is no winner?" One leader responded, "You're kidding me right? Therefore, what you are saying is at the Olympics they do not get a gold medal? All participants get on the stand because they participated?" Members of the leadership team pushed back and said, "There has to be a winner."

I could not back down. It was so clear to me because I had seen and felt it firsthand. As the discussion swirled, there was only one person supporting my idea. For two weeks, I was campaigning for my recommendation and new way of approaching recognition and explaining why it was important. People made fun of me and said, "That is Crazy."

It was truly a challenge until I became curious about their ideas around recognition. What was important to them—winning, be right or being the best. They were not coming from a spirit of cooperation. Finally, the evening came when we had to make a final decision. I stood firm and, in the end, the others supported my recommendation, some with trepidation.

When the first recognition evening arrived, ten employees were honored at a dinner, along with a family member. During the program, managers stood and celebrated each employee, outlining how they had contributed to their department. It was an amazing event and every employee left feeling like a winner. At that moment, no one felt bad or embarrassed and my colleagues understood the value of my idea.

Now, years later, one leader who opposed the idea the most has changed his mind. Today he agrees, "This is one of the most important things we do for our employees on a quarterly, monthly basis."

Everybody sees the value now and agrees there does not have to be a winner.

It took courage not to capitulate because it would have been easy to fold under the pressure. Curiosity helped me gain clarity and courage helped me stand my ground.

Be Curious, Do Clarity, Have Courage.

Curiosity

Leaders are curious. Curiosity is willingness to listen, ask questions, being receptive, accepting and open to possibilities. It starts with personal curiosity determining what is important to you:

> *Who am I?*
> *What are my beliefs and values?*
> *What is my purpose?*
> *What is important to me?*
> *What kind of leader do I want to be?*
> *How can I make a difference?*
> *How do I want others to remember me? (Legacy)*

Getting curious about your purpose, intentions and values allows us to determine who we want to be. Revisit this process regularly as you progress as a leader.

Next, look outside yourself and become curious about others, as I did designing the employee recognition program. Expand your vision seeking connection with colleagues on all levels of the organization. Be open to having conversations with the COO, President, Vice Presidents, Human Resources and others within in the organization ensures you will be driving the correct results. Curiosity almost guarantees alignment with the company's overall vision and mission. Get to know your colleagues, listening and understanding different perspectives.

Talking with others keeps you aware of employee engagement issues, allowing you to fulfill your responsibilities and offer a broader perspective. As leaders, we can get into difficult situations when we have an 'agenda,' think we know everything, and are not willing to listen or ask questions. Consistently seeking to understand those in your organization allows you to create win-win scenarios.

Another aspect of being curious is thinking about what is possible and being open to other options. In training and development, it is my job to influence others to new ways of thinking about and executing tasks. Curiosity is about innovation, learning new things, and looking at future opportunities.

Carol Dweck, author of Mindset, talks about people who have a fixed mindset versus a growth mindset. A "fixed mindset" is when our abilities are predetermined and locked in, where a "growth mindset" is about abilities that can be developed. Curiosity is all about development. It is remembering to ask, "How do we create a win-win through a sense of curiosity?" **Be Curious.**

Clarity

Once we have learned about others, our organization, and ourselves we move to clarity as a leader. While curiosity provides answers, clarity directs the action; the Do. Competences of leadership include knowing who you are, what is important to you, and what you want to create. Authentically decide who you are going to be and what you are willing to do. You may have to discard some beliefs that are not serving you and define your values in detail. True clarity means knowing your purpose, intentions, and values.

Get clear on what is important to you as far as your family, setting boundaries, how you spend your free time, taking care of your body and what you want to do in your environment. Once you are clear about your personal life, gain greater clarity in your professional arena.

Clarity in your career can begin with answering questions such as, "What do I want to contribute? How do I want to grow? How can I make a difference?"

Your level of clarity will determine your ability to lead and influence others. The only way to influence other human beings is by setting the example. Leadership is knowing who you are, what you want to accomplish, and what you are planning for your life or within an organization. When you create clarity and share your goals, it is easier for people to follow you. Having declared and demonstrated where you are going, employees will support you.

Next, clearly communicate your purpose and intentions to the team and share the organization's overall goals and desired results. Clearly defined goals are necessary. Set goals for what you are going to do today, tomorrow, this year, and beyond so you drive the results your organization want to accomplish. As a caution, do not get stuck in your clarity. Continue to revisit the curiosity phase to ensure you are connecting with your team and remain on the most productive path. ***Do Clarity.***

Courage

Leaders behave and decide with courage. Have Courage. Strength and growth only come from continuous effort. Courage is also making hard decisions. Sometimes it takes grit to stay with a project, or walk away from a relationship, a job, or a company.

Courage can be standing up for your needs—be, do and have. Have the courage to take care of yourself; not work 14-hour days, but go home after 8-10 hours so you contribute more the next day. To have courage, you must get out of your comfort zone—that is the only place you will learn anything new. Are you willing to ask for what you want—a raise, a new title, a new job? Perhaps you want to take on a new project or find an innovative way to support the organization. Be courageous and confident asking for resources and support.

Courage is emotional intelligence. Successful leaders surround themselves with talented people. Being the smartest person in the room does not always serve us. Choose to be honest and authentic. Recognize that you may not have all the answers or options. It is always interesting what happens when I say "I don't know, let's find out." This admission allows someone else to rise to the occasion or offer a better solution. When you set an example of courage in this way, it gives others permission to say, "I'm going to be courageous too; I don't have to have all the answers." This creates a safe space for everybody; others thrive and grow when the space is safe.

A true sign of courageous leadership is remaining authentic in difficult situations. Everything is a choice. If you need help, ask, instead of letting your ego get in the way. Your team will support and be encouraged knowing you are not coming from a place of ego or control or manipulation—just true authenticity of what would be the best choice in this moment. ***Have Courage.***

My personal mission statement is "to create and influence through love and encouragement, bringing joy to my life and others." The essence of this is to "Be, Do and Have," focusing on ***Curiosity, Clarity and Courage.***

Leadership requires character and competence—both are important and develop over time from experiences.

Your ability to stay curious, gain clarity and be courageous will not only influence your character, competencies and success, but how others feel about you as well.

Success University for Women™

Success Strategies

① Be willing to change and grow through continuous *Curiosity.*

② Set goals and hold yourself accountable.

③ Have *Courage*—focus on building your confidence. Be willing to take risks.

④ Stay present, come from a place of warmth and always be *Clear* on your intention, power and authority to make things happen.

Notes

Deanna Won

Deanna Won, Founder of Keynotes to Life, is a Speaker, Leadership Consultant, and Holistic Health Coach who inspires people to reach their highest potential through integrating leadership principles with purposeful and healthy living.

A former Air Force Colonel and physicist, Deanna is a graduate of the U.S. Air Force Academy, and has 30 years of leadership experience serving in the US Air Force. Her leadership scenarios are featured at the Stanford Graduate School of Business 'Leadership in Focus' Training.

Deanna received the American Institute of Aeronautics and Astronautics' First Place Award in Public Policy and has been honored as Woman of the Year 2015-2016 by the National Association of Professional Women.

www.deannawon.com

SECTION FOUR: CHAPTER FOUR

Walk in Authenticity

by Deanna Won

> *"Some women are lost in fire. Some women
> are built from it." Michelle K.*

Overcoming Adversity

*"Basics, you have 2 minutes to get in the hallway for formation!"
barked an upperclassman at the U.S. Air Force Academy.*

It was 5:30 am as I scrambled out of bed with my roommates to prepare for our morning run. I was 18 years old and did not know a single person there. Receiving an appointment to attend the highly selective military service academy nestled in the foothills of the Rocky Mountains in Colorado Springs was a prestigious honor. It was also the first time I'd ever left home.

I can still remember the day our postman delivered the official-looking letter containing my Congressional nomination, essentially a four-year scholarship to attend the Academy. Obtaining this nomination felt next to impossible as I did not have any political connections and the acceptance rate was only 18 percent.

I knew I had potential and I felt the need to push myself, making it easier to turn down a four-year scholarship from UC Berkeley. The first Air Force Academy graduating class to include women was only eight years earlier, so remnants of resentment still lingered among male cadets.

While it was physically challenging to compete against my classmates (some of them huge football players), I prepared myself for the typical hazing that occurs at military service academies. Other obstacles would also test my mettle and determination. Was it my imagination...or was I forced to drop for push-ups more than my classmates for no apparent reason? What did I do to deserve this? The hate became brutally evident one day, when an upperclassman snarled in my face, "I'm going to personally make sure that you do not graduate from this place!" When I thought it could not get any worse, an enlisted trainer spit a caustic muddy brown mixture of his chewing tobacco into my eyes, causing them to burn for hours.

On another occasion, I was required to chase an upperclassman running in the rain at full speed while wearing a rain poncho (three sizes too big for me) and carrying an 11-pound rifle. My classmates helplessly watched me tripping over my poncho from the nearby bleachers. Later, my roommate remarked sympathetically, "This goes beyond you just being a woman."

Despite the humiliation, name-calling, and extra abuse, I focused continuously on my goal to graduate and become a commissioned active duty officer and physicist in the United States Air Force. Keeping this purpose forefront in my mind allowed me to not only build up the physical, but also the psychological, and spiritual stamina and fortitude to persist despite the many challenges and obstacles I encountered. At times, I wondered if I would make it.

Four years later, on June 1, 1988, as the Air Force Thunderbird jets roared overhead, I tossed my hat in the air, alongside 1,074 of my fellow classmates on that sunny, warm commencement day. We entered as a class of 1,516 strong, and in spite of attrition, was the first class in years to graduate over a thousand second lieutenants.

For me, it was a jubilant celebration of perseverance, strength, and commitment that would change me forever. This experience provided the foundation of leadership traits that would guide me through not only the next 26 years of my Air Force career, but also the ultimate personal challenge I would face—overcoming cancer.

Support Builds Confidence

At my first assignment at Wright-Patterson Air Force Base in Dayton, Ohio, my supervisor showed me an empty lab room, directing me to "design and build a laser radar system" to detect incoming targets, also providing information on the target's speed and its three-dimensional shape.

While I was thrilled to apply the equations I learned in school in a real-world environment, I felt insecure surrounded by co-workers who were older than me. When I attended and spoke at conferences, most of my colleagues had their PhDs, while I was a brand-new second lieutenant with a bachelor degree. I still remember the day I spoke with my supervisor about my fears, openly expressing to him, "I'm not sure I can do this job..."

"Deanna, I think you will do just fine," he reassured me. As time went on, he continued to give me greater responsibility, involving research on non-mechanical methods for sending laser beams up into space to determine the atmospheric constituents. His simple, encouraging words were the support I needed. His confidence transferred to me, helping me to become more confident in myself and my abilities.

My supervisor's example showed me that as I advanced in leadership responsibilities, I could impact others through encouragement as he had done.

As leaders, we have the power to uplift others through our words and actions.

Taking a Stand for Integrity

On my next assignment, in Melbourne, Florida, I developed novel techniques in detecting chemical, biological, and nuclear warfare agents. As a captain, I was selected to serve on a source selection team to evaluate technical proposals. In the process, I noticed one of the submissions was from a major who was also serving on the source selection team. This was an obvious conflict of interest. Although he outranked me, I could not let the issue rest as I could not resolve this conflict within myself.

Eventually, I went to speak with my supervisor, also a major. He responded by telling me I was "overly sensitive." As time moved on, I continued to feel uncomfortable with this ethical violation. After a great deal of soul-searching and reflection, I concluded that I needed to elevate this issue above my supervisor to the lieutenant colonel, and ultimately the colonel, where I felt sure I was throwing my career away. In spite of feeling these qualms, I was prepared to resign from this position and face the resulting ramifications.

To my surprise, with the lieutenant colonel by my side, the colonel not only agreed with me, but awarded me a Defense Meritorious Service Medal when my assignment ended. This was a rare honor for a captain and reinforced the importance of standing up for one's values. Without integrity, trust cannot exist. Therefore, no matter the situation, integrity should never be compromised.

Leadership by Listening

In my next leadership role, I supervised a division responsible for certifying the flight worthiness of the Titan and Atlas rockets used to launch U.S. national communications, weather, and reconnaissance satellites into space. I quickly discovered that morale was low in the organization, so I set out to determine and address the causes.

One of the issues swirled around a particular individual with a violent nature. At the time, this employee worked on a program to create cost-efficient and standardized launch vehicle components for operating national security space satellites. However, his coworkers complained to me that "he just doesn't carry his weight as an engineer" and they were all afraid of him. I reviewed reports that he would chase employees down the hallway and even try to punch them. I was repeatedly warned to be cautious when dealing with this individual.

However, my personal philosophy has always been to get to know the individual myself, in addition to considering comments from other employees in the organization. As I listened to him share his experience over the years with the organization, I learned that his specialty was in heating, ventilation, and air conditioning. Because of the evolution of the space program, he now found himself being expected to work on sophisticated engineering problems which caused him tremendous stress. Upon listening to him, I realized there was a huge mismatch in his qualifications in comparison with his current duties.

Based on this, I reassigned him as a facilities manager. This new role better utilized his area of expertise, thereby relieving stress and resolving his violent tendencies. Moving this individual also alleviated the resentment and fears of other employees and improved the morale of the organization.

It is important to listen to team members, and to take time to know them as individuals. Always gather information and consider all the different aspects of an issue before making a decision to ensure the most positive outcome for the different stakeholders within the organization. This helps to build trust from your employees, especially when they know that you care and are invested in the organization.

Speaking Your Voice

"True courage is letting go of fears, which frees you to walk in your own authenticity." Deanna Won

As I continued to receive promotions and greater responsibilities in the Air Force, I accepted an assignment developing systems to protect our nation, allies, and troops against biological warfare attacks. While I held this responsibility on a national level, little did I know of the biological challenge engulfing my own body...until I was diagnosed with ovarian cancer. My condition deteriorated to the point where I was admitted into hospice when both my lungs collapsed and filled with fluid. I was given four weeks to live.

Never in my life could I have imagined being in this situation where the specter of death was staring me in the face. However, I had faced adversity before. I believed very strongly in taking an integrative and holistic approach to healing. While it was challenging to question my doctors' recommendations, I felt a deep conviction to voice my desired approach, standing firm on what I would or would not do. I realized that I, alone, had ultimate authority and responsibility over my body and would have to live with the consequences of my decisions. I refused chemotherapy and did not do radiation therapy. With my background in chemical warfare agents, I was aware of the harmful effects of chemotherapy on my immune system. Instead, I focused on strengthening my body with nutrition, addressing emotional wellness, and developing a strong faith. By God's grace, I miraculously survived, and now, 6 years later, I am gratefully thriving.

Sometimes, being a leader is simply having the courage to lead yourself. This is what I call personal leadership. In this situation, I had to speak my voice. There are times in your life when you must speak your voice too.

I trust as you reflect on my life's journey, the common threads that run through my life may run through yours as well. Take some time to think about what you have learned throughout your life. I've shared my experiences here for you as a springboard to success on your journey. If these insights shine a glimmer of light upon your path, then some of the pain and suffering I experienced along the way were not in vain.

*May you have strong convictions
and the courage to act.*

Success University for Women™

Success Strategies

1. *Be willing to take risks.* Be willing to follow your heart's passion to move towards fulfilling your purpose, even if there are inherent risks.

2. *Let go of fear.* By releasing your fears, you create the freedom to accomplish your higher calling and purpose in life.

3. *Focus on your purpose.* Keeping this focus will help you surmount the obstacles and challenges along your path towards success.

4. *Support those around you.* Remind yourself that the people around you are all fellow sojourners along this path of life. As you become aware of others' struggles, make a difference by offering kind support and encouragement whenever you can, one person at a time.

5. *Have confidence.* When self-doubts come, take full ownership of who you are and the value you bring.

Success Strategies

6) *Be transparent.* As you show more of your vulnerability, you allow people around you to better connect and relate to you, which builds trust and confidence.

7) *Hold onto integrity.* In the long run, you have to be at peace with your decisions. Therefore, in any given situation, choose the high road, even if it comes at great cost.

8) *Take time to listen.* Solicit the perspective of the quietest people around you. You may be surprised by what you learn.

9) *Find your authentic voice.* Become aware of that small, still inner voice within you. This is your voice to express because no one else in the world has the same experiences nor the gifts that you have to offer.

10) *Keep the faith.* Faith is what allows you to continue in hope, even when there is no rational reason. Having patience to follow where your faith leads can open the doors to a miraculous outcome you could not have imagined.

Jan Fraser

Authenticity, knowledge and sparkling humor are the magic and motivation Jan brings to her keynotes, training and coaching. With her 35 years in the airline, travel and retail industries, combined with her extensive speaking experience, she is expert in communication, customer service, leadership, sales and success training.

Jan enrolls her audiences to be the best they can be while entertaining them through her unique and engaging speaking style. Her international clients include Fortune 500 companies, schools, governments, and organizations.

Jan is a Certified Canfield Advanced Senior Level Trainer, Professional Success Coach, Author of five books and best-sellers, and Co-Founder of *Success University for Women*™. She is also a member of the National Speakers Association.

www.janfraser.com
www.janfraserbusinesstraining.com

SECTION FOUR: CHAPTER FIVE

Live Lead Legacy

by Jan Fraser

> *"My philosophy is that not only are you responsible for your life, but doing the best at this moment puts you in the best place for the next moment."* Oprah Winfrey

S he had one tooth and, to my amazement, smiled all the time. I met her while speaking at a conference in Louisville, Kentucky, sponsored by the Catholic Church. Each of the attendees had experienced torture, rape, maiming, or other heinous acts in their native countries and had escaped to America to start a new life.

My speaking topic that day was 'Self-Empowerment' and adjusting to their new lives in America.

I felt as if I were speaking at the United Nations with audience members from all over the world. Attendees wore native dress and brought food from their homeland to share.

Six translators were tasked with conveying my message in native tongues, but were not able to speak the languages of all of the women present. I dressed in my 'salwar kameez' I had bought on a six-week training trip to India, as I wanted to support these women and give them the respect they deserved.

I was honored by the opportunity to speak, and overwhelmed by the task.

How could I, a middle-class woman from Ohio, stand on a stage and influence these women who had endured unimaginable pain and suffering in their native lands?

During my presentation, I paused after each phrase, allowing the translators to quickly speak my message in their native tongues. Some of the women shared their stories of anguish with the group. I was profoundly moved. The courageous stories of these women who had come to America dreaming of a better life echoed through the ballroom and reached me at my core.

As I spoke, I noticed a tall woman who carried herself with grace and elegance proudly wearing a dress and head wrap ablaze with a colorful African pattern. She sat patiently throughout the morning session. She smiled up at me unabashedly throughout my talk, despite having only one solitary upper tooth in her mouth. I was riveted to her beautiful face. Joy and light seemed to emanate from her despite the tragedies she had surely experienced in her life.

After the first break, the Swahili translator approached me, with the African woman possessing one tooth. She explained that the woman was Ethiopian, and since there was no Ethiopian translator available, the Swahili language was her closest dialect. The translator said, "The lady from Ethiopia wanted me to tell you, that she doesn't understand a word you are saying and yet she is happy to be here with you today. She is hopeful for a better future because of you."

I looked past the translator and into the eyes of the Ethiopian woman. She recognized my unconditional love and looked to me as a leader, knowing I supported her and her dreams. I embraced my new friend for a long time. I communicated that she had made a difference in my life too.

I keep a photograph of the women from that conference as a reminder that we do not, at times, recognize the different ways we influence others.

> *"Everyone is influencing the people around them one way or another."* Robin S. Sharma

We Influence in Many Ways

As leaders, we influence everyone who comes into our sphere. In this experience, I was able to infuse this woman with hope, even though she didn't understand my words. We influence by our focused attention, communication, either verbal or non-verbal, image, body language, support and dedicated time.

My friend, Forrest, has an amazing focus. After suffering two traumatic brain injuries, he relearned how to speak, write and walk. When he is speaking to you, you are the only person that matters in that moment. His clarity and concentration make the listener feel important. Forrest has evolved into a motivational speaker who influences and touches lives daily with his magnetic focus.

Speaking at my first Women's Conference, my co-facilitators helped me see how I could create greater influence with my audience through my image. They remarked that my two-piece church outfit was not appropriate for a business conference for women.

They asked me if I wanted to be successful in my keynote speaking. I told them I did. They said, "Lose the outfit." Their feedback worked for me as now I wear a suit jacket with pants or a skirt to set an example for professional working women.

Through our daily communication and behavior, we influence intentionally and unintentionally, positively and negatively. The ***Influence Grid™*** I created visually represents these different aspects:

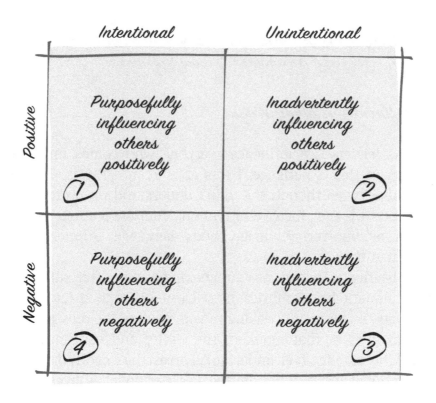

My goal is to help other leaders be more aware of how they are influencing people. Increasing awareness can illuminate what you are doing that works, and where you need to adjust your focus. At times, leaders don't realize how unintentional words and actions affect those around them.

Start with an exercise.

Observe yourself and how you interact with others for a day or even a week. Step outside yourself and see your communication from an external perspective. Ask a trusted colleague or friend to be your eyes and ears. Keep the ***Influence Grid*™** with you and make notes of the different situations you encounter and the results. Clues to your leadership approach can be found in employee reactions, effectiveness, buy-in, productivity and morale.

Answer these questions:

* How am I treating people?
* How am I speaking to others?
* How do others react when I discuss a situation or give them a task?
* What is the feeling in the room when I leave?

Consider these clues:

* Are people willing to trust and follow my direction?
* Could I be abrasive without knowing it?
* What is the usual reaction to my communication?
* Are people backing away from or talking about me in a negative way?

Your answers will tell you how you are influencing others in your leadership communication and behavior.

If you find that you are in **Quadrant One** most of the time, congratulations! Keep up the good work. Celebrate yourself and the way you are leading your team. If you found that most of your influence is unintentional, set a goal to be more intentional and aware of the ways you affect others.

On the other hand, if you are surprised to find your communication in **Quadrants Three** or **Four,** you are influencing your team in a negative way. You can offend without realizing it. Make a decision to get intentional about how you are leading and step into a positive **Quadrant One** or **Two** approach. If necessary, find a mentor or coach who can assist you. Immersing yourself in positive reading like *Success University for Women™* books or motivational CD's will be a start. Surround yourself with positive peers and leaders. Both you and your team will be amazed at the changes when you begin leading in a positive way.

In **Quadrant Four** we find leaders who are intentionally negative with others. Leaders in this group often believe there is only one-way to lead: bluntly or harshly. Perhaps, this is the only leadership model you have known. You can change your approach. Fear is not the only way to get others to follow you; connection, encouragement and positivity work, while creating an atmosphere of trust and respect. Each work environment has a unique population and goal structure and leadership styles may need to be adjusted.

If your leadership efforts are concentrated in the negative zone, I invite you revisit *'Section One: Transforming'* of this book and find ways to change your approach. Successful leaders remain in the positive area in their communication, writing, and non-verbal body language. They know that positivity on their part creates greater connection with others and productivity within teams.

"I suppose leadership at one time meant muscles; but today it means getting along with people."
Indira Gandhi

Importance of Connection

When first working as a customer service agent for Delta Air Lines in San Diego, California, I could not get a full-time position. This station due to its temperate climate was a magnet for senior full time staff. For three years I worked as a 'Temporary Part-Time' employee or TPT. While working there, I discovered the Delta slogan, "You're part of the Delta family." I approached my position, though part time, with gusto, feeling like I was 'part of the family.'

As a baggage service agent, I created the first ever Delta Air Lines employee baggage delivery system, where employees delivered baggage on their way home to Delta customers whose bags had been delayed. I won the 'Feather in Your Cap' award from the president of Delta Air Lines for outstanding customer service. I enjoyed my job, was motivated to contribute, and felt like I was a valued member of the Delta family.

Our team gained a new station manager and during a conversation in his office I asked him about the possibility of becoming a full-time employee. His response was, "You know being a TPT, you are not part of the Delta family." Ouch. It hit me like a ton of bricks. At this point I realized he did not know me. He did not know how devoted I was to the team, working holidays, covering co-workers' shifts and creatively solving issues at the station. He didn't know about the baggage delivery system, my good customer letters or my awards. I said to myself, "He doesn't care about me. No matter what I do, I don't matter to him or this company.'" When employees do not feel appreciated, valued or connected, they question their commitment to the team or the job.

As soon as I clocked out that day, I went straight to my friends at the American Airlines ticket counter and inquired about a flight attendant position, with American, which I later acquired. I became a valuable employee to American Airlines and I could have been that for Delta. If that leader had taken the time to check my file, talk to me, discover how passionate I was about customer service, or appreciate my efforts in any way, he would not have made that **Quadrant Four** statement. He was likely functioning in the unintentional, negative quadrant. He did not know how his words cut me down and severed any connection we may have had.

> *Leaders can create relationships that empower teams and individuals or not.*

If employees sense that their supervisor, manager, or leader is invested in their success by communicating positively the team blooms and prospers. If they sense that there is no connection, support, or caring on the part of their leader, they shrink from the job and look for ways to disappear on breaks or leave that job permanently. When there is an atmosphere of positivity, understanding and support, team members are motivated to follow the leader and give their all.

In your role, work to develop a relationship with those you lead so that you are in a position to influence and empower them. Consciously create connections.

Legacy

I never met my ex-husband's wife and yet I saved her life.

Larry and I were divorced when our daughters were small and we lost contact over the years. I heard he married Barbara and I was happy for him.

Thirty-one years later, I learned the sad news that Larry passed away from pancreatic cancer. I reached out in sympathy to Barbara. Her email reply took me by surprise. Overcome with grief at losing the love of her life, she was contemplating suicide. I was shocked and jumped into action.

Barbara was a registered nurse, with valuable skills and the expertise to help others. I knew she still had life inside her. Neither Larry nor Barbara knew I had become an author and motivational speaker. I asked permission (via email) to send her one of my books that I hoped would provide encouragement. The book contained a story about a friend of mine who was able to move on after losing her husband because she knew she still had work to do. Barbara replied that I could send her my book.

I did not get a response for two weeks and I was afraid she had followed through on her plan to commit suicide. Thankfully, when Barbara's email finally arrived, she told me she had been crying for two hours after reading a story in my book. However, it wasn't the story I thought it would be. It was a story I wrote about soulmates that touched her. She realized that she needed to find another dream and move forward after Larry's death.

I saved Barbara's life.

We may never know the impact we have on people we meet from small interactions to possibly saving lives.

Choose to intentionally influence others positively.
You decide the legacy you leave.

Success University for Women™

Success Strategies

1. Be the leader others want to follow. Be the leader you would want to follow.

2. Consistently seek to appreciate and value others.

3. Be intentionally positive. Refer to the *Influence Grid™* for source.

4. When someone is talking with you, listen with 100% of your focus.

5. Connect positively with others to build your legacy.

Congratulations
GRADUATE!

To obtain your Certificate of Achievement, please email us at *certificate@successuniversityforwomen.com* with the words 'Certificate SUW3' in the subject line. We'll email you your Certificate and keep you up-to-date on upcoming events in *Success University for Women*™.

The photo on the previous page and cover photo were taken at Success University for Women™ Conference in Hamilton, Bermuda on April 30, 2017. Photo Credit: Joe Marable.

CERTIFICATE OF ACHIEVEMENT

WOMEN IN LEADERSHIP

LEVEL THREE

You have successfully completed Level Three
of the *Success University for Women*™ curriculum.
Implement the strategies you have learned
to influence others positively, and embark on a
more significant leadership role!

Co-Founders, *Success University for Women*™

Jan Fraser   Catherine Scheers

Success University for Women™

Success University for Women™ *Curriculum*

Want more success in your life? Now that you've finished this book (Level Three of our 'curriculum'), keep the momentum going with *Success University for Women*™ Conferences, upcoming online courses, and upcoming volumes.

Success University for Women™ *Conferences*

Need a motivational 'shot-in-the-arm' or a 'kick in your determination?' Want to meet the Co-Creators of *Success University for Women*™ and connect with the authors? You won't want to miss the rewarding *Success University for Women*™ Conferences. Held in exciting cities around the world, these conferences bring together our authors and readers—women who will inspire and uplift you and help you to succeed in life! You'll benefit from keynote speakers, breakout working sessions, and networking with wise women from around the world! Check our website for upcoming dates and locations: *www.successuniversityforwomen.com*

Success University for Women™ *Invitation*

Do you want to be an author in an upcoming *Success University for Women*™ book? Are you a successful woman intentionally creating positive ripples and have an inspirational message to share with the world?

Contact us at *submit@successuniversityforwomen.com* with the words 'SUW Writer Proposal' in the subject line to share your inspiring success stories. You may become a contributor in one of our upcoming volumes.

Success University for Women™

Success University for Women™ Book Series

Check out our complete series of *Success University for Women*™ books to build on your success!

What do 24 winning women from 11 countries on 3 continents with careers as varied as Chef, Lawyer, Farmer, Speaker, Commercial Pilot, Accountant, Fitness Cover Model, Entrepreneur, and Life Coach have in common? **Success University for Women™!** Let this book be your virtual Life Coach—it's like having all of these exceptional women on your team, right by your side, as you travel through life's challenges.

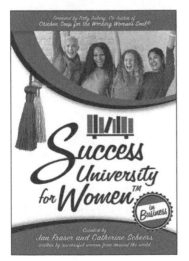

It has been said that experience is the best teacher. But it can also be painful—it's better to benefit from others' journeys. That's the premise of **Success University for Women™ in Business.** You'll gain wisdom from the stories of our Success Sisters—16 authors living in 7 countries around the world. They bravely share their tears and triumphs on their journeys to master the world of business.